YO-BZZ-216

THE LARGE
MEMBERSHIP CHURCH

WARREN J. HARTMAN
ROBERT L. WILSON

DISCIPLESHIP RESOURCES
MATERIALS FOR GROWTH IN CHRISTIAN FAITH AND LIFE
P.O. Box 189 • Nashville, TN 37202 • Phone (615) 340-7285

To Lyle E. Schaller
Our friend and
America's foremost church
consultant

ISBN 0-88177-075-2

Library of Congress Catalog Card No. 89-50428

DR075B

CONTENTS

PREFACE

Throughout the Christian era the church has been structured in a variety of ways to communicate its message. The gospel may remain the same, but the social setting in which it is proclaimed has varied widely. The manner in which a church organizes itself depends on the larger community of which it is a part. When the society changes, the church too has altered its method and structure to effectively proclaim its message. Certain types of religious organizations were in their time highly effective in bringing the message of Christ to the people. The Baptist farmer-preachers founded congregations in rural communities across the land. These were served by what today we would call bi-vocational pastors. Methodist circuit riders enabled that denomination to keep pace with a westward-moving population. The Methodist pastor traveled throughout his assigned territory preaching and supervising the local pastors who carried on the daily work of the congregations on the charge. As America became more urban, the denominations established neighborhood churches in the developing cities. These were located to serve the residents of a particular neighborhood and were placed so that many of the members could conveniently walk to church.

Many of the churches which were established as the frontier was being settled still continue in rural areas. Every city has a large number of small to medium-size neighborhood congregations which today may or may not primarily serve the residents of communities in which they are located. These churches continue to minister in significant ways, but they represent a continuation of a denominational strategy designed for another era. Church leaders of today who have responsibility for establishing new churches are not attempting to start small rural congregations or medium-size urban neighborhood churches.

The question which must be asked and satisfactorily answered is what type of religious organization today will be most effective in presenting the gospel, helping people understand the Christian faith, and providing opportunities for them to minister in the name of Christ. *It is our contention that the large church is the form of religious organization which may be to the late twentieth century what the rural circuit and village church were to the early nineteenth century and the urban neighborhood congregation was to the first half of the twentieth century.*

We are aware that a substantial majority of Protestant congregations are small. Somewhere between one-half and two-thirds have fewer than 200 members on the roll. Approximately one-half average fewer than 100 persons at worship. While these churches render significant service, there are indications that a substantial proportion of denominational growth is occurring in large churches. Virtually every city has seen the development of what might be termed mega-churches. These large congregations which occupy campus-like facilities have constituencies which numbers in the thousands. Some are affiliated with a denomination; others are independent. Such churches are certain to have an increasing influence on the presentation of the Christian message in the period immediately ahead.

The development of the mega-church is consistent with trends in American society. Many members of today's older generation, i.e., those over sixty, grew up in rural and small town communities. A large proportion had firsthand experience with life on the farm. They either have lived on a farm or had parents, grandparents, or other relatives who did. They also may have in their youth attended a small rural church.

Many of the present generation of young adults have not had such experiences. They are more likely to have grown up in a metropolitan area. Many are products of the suburban communities which were developed in the period following World War II. Their experience has been in large institutions. Their education was received in large schools. Even if they lived in a rural area or small town, the probability that they attended a consolidated school is high. They make their purchases in the large shopping malls. And if they participated in a church when they were growing up, it was more likely to have been a large congregation which offered a wider range of programs than the churches their parents attended. The result is a generation which expects a variety of choices for themselves and their families among the available goods and services. This expectation also includes the programs offered by the local church. Such persons today tend to be attracted to the large church with its specialized multiple staff and variety of activities.

This is a book about the large church. We define the large church as a congregation with an average attendance of more than 350 persons at the Sunday worship service. Not more than one church in ten falls into this category. There are differences among large churches of different sizes. However, the congregation with an average worship attendance of 400 has more in common with one with 2,000 worshipers every Sunday than either does with a church averaging 75 people each week.

In the pages that follow, we shall be looking at the role of the large church in Protestantism today, trends in such congregations, the relationship of the large church to its parent denomination, the senior pastor and the staff. Attention will be given to the program or what is happening in these churches. Finally, the task of managing a large church will be considered.

All of the congregations included in this study are predominantly white. There are many outstanding large black churches in many denominations. The large black congregations are sufficiently different from their white counterparts that generalizations about one do not necessarily apply to the other. A study of large black churches needs to be the subject of a subsequent research project by someone with expertise in black religious institutions.

The authors are United Methodist pastors and admittedly write from the perspective of that denomination. However, the study was not limited to that denomination but included churches of other communions as well as independent congregations. In today's world, large churches of different denominations are more alike than small and large churches of the same denomination.

The cooperation of many people made this project possible. The authors wish to express their appreciation to the pastors, staff, and members who generously gave their time and provided the information on which this book is based. A number of persons read and commented on the manuscript. A special thanks is due Douglas W. Johnson, Ezra Earl Jones, Lyle E. Schaller, and Alan K. Waltz for their insights, encouragement, and critiques as the study progressed, and to Ginny Ashmore of the J. M. Ormond Center who assisted with the research and prepared the manuscript.

Finally we want to say a word about language. When referring to the senior pastors, we use masculine terms. It is not that we are insensitive to inclusive language, but it is because all of the senior pastors of the large churches in our study were men. There were ordained women on the staff of many churches which we studied, but none were senior pastors.

It is our hope that this book will be of value to those clergy and lay persons who proclaim the gospel in and perform their ministries through the large membership church.

Warren J. Hartman
Nashville, Tennessee

Robert L. Wilson
Durham, North Carolina

1. THE LARGE CHURCH IN PROTESTANTISM

The typical large church is located on a major street in an outlying section of a large city or in one of its suburbs. Its impressive building was erected after 1960. It is set on a well-landscaped campus which includes vast expanses of parking designed to conveniently accommodate the hundreds of attendees. The building may range from traditional to modern in style, but it is unmistakably a church. A prominent sign tells passers-by the church's denomination and hours of the major worship services and the Sunday school. The name of the senior pastor is usually included.

The entrances to the parking areas are clearly marked. The size of the parking lot indicates that one could attend without having any difficulty finding a space for the car. It is also evident that this congregation does not anticipate that anyone will walk to church.

The large membership church is not a new phenomenon; there have been such congregations throughout the twentieth century. New in the 1980s is the development of the mega-church and the increasingly important role which such institutions are playing in the religious life of large numbers of Christian people.

What Is Meant by Large

To be considered large for the purpose of this study, a church must have an average attendance at the Sunday morning worship service(s) of 350 persons or more. This is based on the assumption that a congregation has an average attendance equal to approximately one-third of the members. Average attendance was used rather than the number of people on the roll because the accuracy of church records varies somewhat. Furthermore, there are some variations among denominations in their definition of membership. Average attendance, however, represents actual participants.

The average attendance of 350 or more represents congregations with memberships of over 1,000. Admittedly this is an arbitrary figure, but it includes a small number of the largest congregations (for example, only 3.7 percent of all United Methodist congregations report 1,000 or more members). These are churches which, in addition to the pastor, have

1

other staff members. They offer a range of programs designed for different age and interest groups. We consider such churches large.

There are, of course, more congregations in the 1,000 to 2,000 membership range than over 2,000. United Methodism has 1,125 in the smaller category and 235 in the larger. Of these, 59 have more than 3,000 members. We refer to these as mega-churches. Church members may perceive their church differently. For example, a congregation with an average worship attendance of 375 may not consider itself large. Such a church, however, has much in common with one averaging 1800 worshipers. There will be somewhat fewer activities and a smaller staff in the smaller church than in the larger. However both will be obviously different from the congregation with 65 in attendance.

The Development of the Large Church

Large congregations were made possible when the nation became urbanized. As the cities increased in size and number, there were concentrations of people who could become members of large churches. Such congregations were first located in the center of the city. The railroad and trolley systems made the central business district accessible. As technology made rapid transit more efficient, it became possible for persons to live further out and still work, shop, and worship downtown.

The very large churches had not developed by the turn of the century. A large number of Methodist congregations with between 200 and 400 members were located in the major cities. Philadelphia had no Methodist church of over 776 members and only four congregations out of 92 had over 700 members. New York had only one large church. Similar patterns existed in Chicago and Detroit. In 1900 Detroit had only two large Methodist congregations, the largest with 960 members. Detroit's growth was to come later with the development of the auto industry. Chicago had six large churches with memberships ranging from 739 to 2906.

By 1925 the development of better transit systems and the appearance of the automobile made it convenient for persons to travel farther to church. Detroit had one Methodist church of 3,065 members and two others with over 2,000 adherents. Another trend was noticeable by 1925. The large congregations were appearing in outlying areas. Many of these were within the city limits, but they were in areas then being developed. These were the sections into which the middle class and upwardly mobile people were moving. The Englewood and Austin sections of Chicago and the Mount Airy section of Philadelphia are examples.

By the 1950s the large churches tended toward increasing numbers in the suburban areas, although many were still within the central cities. The vast migration to the cities of Southern blacks which began during World War II continued after hostilities ceased. The racially changing community was a factor in virtually every city, with the result that many white neighborhoods became black. This resulted in the relocation of many Anglo congregations, usually preceded by a period of membership decline. There were still some large white congregations in the central cities, but, increasingly, the large membership churches located there are black.

By the mid 1980s the large white congregations were in the more remote suburbs. Only two United Methodist churches in Chicago had more than 1,000 members. Only one church in Detroit, two in Philadelphia, and four in New York had over 1,000 members. Of these eight churches, six are black. In some of the Southern cities such as Charlotte and Richmond, the large churches are still within the city limits because that is where development continues to occur. In some of the smaller cities which have not grown rapidly, particularly in the South, the downtown church has remained strong with a membership of 1,000 to 1,500.

These trends have important implications for denominational strategy. For almost two decades in the late 1960s and 1970s, relatively few new churches were organized in the mainline denominations. Recently there has been an increase in interest and activity in new church development. Several judicatories are involved in major financial campaigns to underwrite the cost of starting new congregations. Denominational leaders must ask what type of congregations the proposed new churches are expected to be. Will they be planned, and located on a site secured so they can develop into large congregations? Will the denominations plan yesterday's churches and expect them to effectively witness and minister into the twenty-first century?

It is a difficult task to establish institutions in a continually changing society. It is vital that those who make the critical decision have a clear vision of the kind of church into which the new congregation is expected to develop. Only then can the decisions be made that will make this goal possible.

The Importance of the Large Church

The large church occupies an exceedingly important place in the religious life of many people. Although there are relatively few large congregations compared to the number of small ones, they have a large proportion of the members and the worshipers. An examination of United Methodist data illustrate this fact.

There were, as of December 31, 1987, only 59 mega-churches with over 3,000 members or 0.2 percent of the total churches. In contrast, 7,609 churches have fewer than 50 members. These 59 mega-churches contain 2.9 percent of the denomination's total membership, while the more than 7,000 small churches have 2.5 percent of the members. There are 34,436 more members in the 59 mega-churches than in 7,609 small ones.

The large churches tend to be located in the Southeast and South Central sections of the country. United Methodism in 1986 had 507 congregations in which the attendance at worship averaged 500 or more. Of these, 70 percent were in the Southeast and South Central regions.

The United Methodist Church has 1,347 congregations or 3.7 percent of the total with more than 1,000 members. It has 16,105 churches with fewer than 100 members representing 42.7 percent of the total. These 1,347 large churches have 23.8 percent of the total membership of the entire denomination while 9.3 percent of the total members are in the 16,105 smallest churches. A similar trend can be noted in attenders where on an average Sunday the 3.7 percent of the congregations of over 1,000 members have 19.3 percent of the worshipers, while the 42.7 percent of the churches of under 100 members have 13.4 percent.

While a large proportion of the total attenders are in the relatively few large churches, the smaller congregations do have a higher proportion of the members attending than do the large ones. For example, the worship attendance averages 55.6 percent of the membership for congregations with fewer than 100 members but only 30.9 percent for those with over 1,000 members. There is more pressure on the person in a small church to be present because his or her presence is essential for the congregation to function. A higher percentage of those who attend small membership churches tend to be directly related to one another in several primary or face-to-face group settings than large church attenders. When they miss an activity in the church, others notice their absence and often inquire about them. In most large churches, there is much less peer pressure to attend the worship services.

The large church is an important source of funds for the benevolence program and administrative expenses of the denomination. Even with the costs of a big staff, local programs, and maintenance of the building, the large churches are able to provide substantial support for causes outside the congregation. The 59 largest United Methodist churches provide over $14 million for the denomination's administrative costs and programs. This includes the apportioned funds, all other benevolent programs, and the work of the United Methodist Women. Thus 0.2 percent of the congregations and 2.9 percent of the members are providing 4.2 percent of the denomination's expenses and benevolences.

Types of Large Churches

There are two basic types of large churches. The first are those which are affiliated with one of the recognized denominations. They may be Lutheran, Baptist, United Methodist, or Assembly of God. Because of their size and strength, they tend to have some degree of independence from the denomination. However, they are clearly identified with a particular denomination and are a major source of support for the mission programs of the parent body. Their clergy will have their credentials from the denomination.

Among the denominational large churches there are two variations. The first is the congregation which by virtue of the community from which its members come, the quality of its program, and its pastoral leadership has grown to be a large church. It clearly represents the generally accepted theological and social perspective of the denomination. The congregation supports the mission program and is perceived to be one of the denomination's most important churches.

The second variety of large church is one that is in some way deviant from the denominational norm. While it is clearly a congregation of its denomination, it has some points of difference with the parent body. These are not serious enough to result in separation, but there can at times be tensions. It may represent a more conservative theological perspective; it may be charismatic. Its support of denominational causes may be selective, with more support going to specific projects with which the congregation is in agreement and a minimal amount designated for the officially approved causes.

There are also some congregations which are liberal or even radical and thus deviant from the denominational norm. Examples would be churches involved in the Sanctuary Movement or the congregation which invited Daniel Ortega, the President of Nicaragua, to preach. These, however, tend to be churches with relatively small memberships and do not attract large numbers of adherents.

The second type of large churches are independent congregations which are not responsible to any parent body. No group exercises supervision or control over them. They may have been affiliated with a denomination at one time but have disassociated themselves for any number of reasons. Two of the most common reasons are related to the former denomination or to the pastor. They may have disagreed with some denominational polity or they may have felt that the prevailing theological climate in the denomination was no longer acceptable to them, so they severed their denominational ties. A second cluster of reasons that are given for disassociating with a denomination are traceable to the pastor's differences with the denomination. Not only does the pastor withdraw, but he takes a sizable number of the congregation with him and forms a new church. Many of the congregations that withdrew from the Presbyterian denomination in the past decade were theologically conservative.

Other congregations have never been part of a denomination. These congregations frequently include some reference to their independence in the names by which they are known. Terms such as Interdenominational Fellowship, Independent Church of . . . , Bible Fellowship Chapel, Evangel Temple, or Faith Church indicate their independent status.

One noticeable characteristic of almost every large independent congregation is the aggressive manner by which they publicize their church. They utilize a variety of means. Newspaper ads, highway billboards, radio and TV spot announcements, radio and TV broadcasts of services are commonly used by the large independent congregations. Most have developed a large mailing list which they use regularly to maintain contact with members and prospective members.

The clergy may have received their ordination from a variety of bodies or have been ordained by the congregation itself. While ministerial leadership is a critical factor in all large churches, the big independent congregations tend to owe their development to a particular individual. Such institutions may continue beyond the founding pastor, but all seem to have been the result of the work of a particular individual.

There are both differences and similarities between the large denominational churches and the big independent congregations. These will be discussed throughout the book.

Factors in the Development of the Large Church

Seven factors determine if a particular congregation will become large. All of these are important and have a bearing on the development of the church.

The first factor is the community context. Obviously there must not only be an adequate population from which the congregation can draw members but it must be a population which has a sufficiently high proportion of persons who are sympathetic with the theological position of the congregation. In practical terms this means a location in an urban area where there are enough residents who can conveniently travel to the church.

The expectation is not only attendance on Sunday morning but participation for different members of the family at other times during the week. The teenager may return on Sunday evening for a meeting of the youth fellowship. There will be study groups, prayer meetings, sessions of the governing board and various committees, and choir rehearsals throughout the week. The pattern of participation by the average member is such that he or she must be able to get to the church without spending so much time in transit that attendance at the various functions is discouraged.

A second factor in the development of the large church is its location. It must be in a place that is visible and accessible. Most large churches are on a major street where they are seen by the thousands of persons who pass by daily. It has been said that if it is necessary to have a sign to show people how to get to a church, the church should have been placed where the sign is.

Large churches tend to draw persons from a wide area, often from throughout the metropolitan area. Nevertheless the location still has an impact on who attends. One large independent church with an average attendance of just under 3000 moved from a site near the center of the city to a location adjacent to an expressway on the edge of the city. One of the pastors observed that people were having to drive out to the church. However, he expects the area beyond the church to be developed in the foreseeable future, which he feels "will provide this congregation with an opportunity for significant growth."

Related to location is the third factor, facilities. The church building tells something ideal about the nature of the congregation and what goes on there. It makes a statement to all who pass by. Are the facilities inviting to nonmembers? Some church signs carry only the name and denomination, i.e., Asbury United Methodist Church or St. Paul's Lutheran Church, but give no information concerning the times of worship or other activities. What message does this convey?

The style and condition of the physical plant give an indication of what happens there and the kinds of people who attend. A large auditorium suggests an emphasis on preaching. A large educational facility indicates that importance is given to the Sunday school. A preschool or a day school shows another emphasis. A family life center signals the importance attached to a family ministry. A youth building or a senior citizens center shows other emphases.

A fourth factor in the development of a large congregation is its ability to develop an appropriate response to the varying needs of different groups of people. Such a church is perceived to have something significant to offer which merits the time, energy, and support of the members. A function of religion is to provide meaning for life, to help people make sense out of their experiences, and to deal with the multitude of problems they have to face from time to time.

The church provides a frame of reference for the individual's understanding of how he or she fits into the scheme of things. This happens in any congregation regardless of its size. The unique aspect of the large church is that it can provide ministries to a wide range of groups of persons who have particular interests and needs at certain times in their lives. Examples would include single young adults, young families with small children, single parents, senior citizens, retarded persons, etc. Such persons can find help and mutual support from people in similar circumstances. Because of the number of persons involved in a large church, there are enough people to form groups to deal with a variety of specific needs. One of the attractions of the large church is the range of its programs which enable individuals to find activities which are relevant to them at a particular time. A strong and varied weekday program tends to attract newcomers, particularly persons born after 1945.

A fifth factor in the development of the large church is leadership. While all factors are important, none is of greater significance than leadership. There are three types of leaders in every large church. The first is the senior pastor. This is the person who articulates the vision and helps the congregation define its goals and purposes. The senior pastor tends to be not only the chief executive officer but a symbol of the congregation itself. The pastor is not only identified with the church but the church with the pastor.

The second group of leaders includes the professional staff members. These are the persons responsible for the many aspects of the church's program. They direct the educational and music programs and provide leadership for the special interest groups. The day-to-day and week-to-week programs are the responsibility of these leaders. To a great degree their skill determines the effectiveness of the church.

The third group of leaders includes the lay members who chair and staff the committees and do the volunteer work required in any congregation. These are the persons who catch the vision articulated by the pastor and who support the staff with their time, talent, and money. An effective church must have all three types of leaders.

The sixth factor is timing. A large church requires that a congregation be organized at the right time in the right community and have the right leadership. Effectiveness depends on the convergence of several critical factors at the same time. A church can be organized before a community begins to develop or be established after an area has been developed and many residents already affiliated with churches. It can be organized at the appropriate time and place but not have the kind of leadership needed. The ability to take action at the right time may be perceived as good planning or the guidance of the Holy Spirit. It is, however, an essential factor for the development of a large church.

A seventh factor which is somewhat difficult to define is the attitude of the members. Some congregations never become large because the people never perceive their potential as a large church. Some congregations which are quite large continue to see themselves as a small membership church. The perception of the people concerning the nature and role of their church is critical.

Issues for the Large Church

In the period immediately ahead, those persons responsible for large churches will be confronted with several issues which will have a significant effect on the development and effectiveness of these congregations.

The first is the understanding of what the local church is to be and to do. These are the theological assumptions about the nature and purpose of the congregation and how the people relate to the pastor. Some Lutherans, for example, feel that the congregation should not exceed a number beyond which it is impossible for the pastor to know and give oversight to each of the members. When a church has many over 400 members, the number is considered too large for one pastor to know all the members well. It is critical that the goals of the church be clear so that institutional forms can be developed which are consistent with these goals and which can be evaluated in terms of their effectiveness.

A second issue is leadership, particularly pastoral leadership. This includes the senior pastor and the members of the staff, both ordained and unordained. Clergy are trained to be generalists. Seminaries necessarily provide basic theological education. They do not train pastors to serve in particular types of churches. It is probably too early for students to specialize, but the individual must learn skills to apply seminary training to particular types of churches. The successful large church pastor, like the effective rural church pastor, is largely self-taught.

Thus large churches and the denomination must determine what kinds of leaders are needed. This includes the senior pastor and the members of the church staff. Only when the required skills are understood can appropriate persons be found and the necessary training be provided.

A third issue is the role of the large church in its parent denomination. The large majority of congregations in Protestantism have relatively small memberships, and the majority of pastors serve one or sometimes more than one small church. In the various regional legislative bodies, a majority of votes are cast by persons affiliated with small or medium-sized congregations. Judicatory actions may be geared toward the issues and needs of the small or medium-size congregations. The problems and concerns of the large churches may be overlooked.

A fourth issue is the image that the pastor and members of the church have of their congregation. One of the most rapidly growing United Methodist churches has always seen itself as a large church. When the church was started a few years ago, the pastor did not hold the first worship service until he was confident that there would be at least 200 in attendance. The members of large churches think of their congregation as large. Everything about them is designed for growth and expansion. They are staffed for growth. They are constantly establishing new groups around a variety of interests and for distinct and identifiable groups of persons in the community and congregation. Different styles of leadership for such groups are utilized. When a group does not engender the anticipated response, little effort is spent trying to keep it alive. It is allowed to disband and other groups are established which are more in keeping with the needs and interests of persons in the congregation and community.

There is the feeling among some clergy that the large church is a strong institution that does not have the problems of the small congregation. This is only correct in part. The problems the large church faces are different from those of the small, but they can be no less difficult or serious. The large church can be a highly vulnerable institution in ways that the small church is not. Since a greater proportion of the lay members are in large congregations, the role of these churches and their strengths and problems must be understood by all concerned.

2. THE MEMBERS OF THE LARGE CHURCH

The church is made up of persons who are followers of Christ. A congregation is the people who gather for worship and study, who represent the church through service and witness, and who contribute the funds which provide for the local expenses and for the broader ministries of the church beyond the local community. This chapter will focus on the members of large churches. It will consider such questions as: the age distribution of members and how this compares to the general population, the types of families represented in the membership, and what people like and dislike about large churches.

While local churches are both similar and different, there are clear differences between large and small congregations. In contrast, there are often greater similarities between two large membership churches of different denominations than there are between two congregations of the same denomination but with different size memberships. It is not uncommon for senior pastors of large churches to meet regularly. The same holds for the lay persons who are in those churches. The members of a large United Methodist church may have more in common with the members of a nearby large Presbyterian, or Baptist, or Assembly of God congregation than they have in common with those from other small United Methodist churches in the same city.

The primary data on which this chapter is based were gathered by surveying approximately 1200 United Methodist churches. These data were supplemented by extensive interviews with the senior pastor, staff members, and other persons in a number of large membership churches in other denominations, and in large independent churches.

Age of Members

While The United Methodist Church does not gather data on the age distributions of members, an estimate was secured of the ages of all persons who regularly attend one or more activities at least once a month in the congregations surveyed. Those data are not comprehensive, but the results from different churches were similar and therefore presumed to be reliable.

11

The ages of the participants in large churches and all churches were compared with the age distribution of the US population as reported by the US Bureau of Census. Table I shows the age distribution in 1986 of active lay persons for United Methodist churches of all sizes, the age distribution of lay persons in large membership churches, and the age distribution of the United States population.

TABLE I

Age Distribution of Active United Methodist Lay Persons by Church Membership Size Compared with US Population by Percent

Age Group	Laity in all UM churches	Laity in Large UM churches	US Population
11 and under	16.5	14.4	16.7
12 to 18	9.4	11.1	10.8
19 to 29	8.1	11.5	19.7
30 to 39	11.7	9.3	15.9
40 to 49	13.7	11.4	10.9
50 to 64	19.3	20.8	13.9
65 and over	21.3	21.5	12.1

When both distributions of United Methodist lay persons are compared with the United States census data, two significant differences can be noted. First, the number of persons who are between 19 and 39 years of age are under-represented in the church membership and those above 50 years are over-represented. Second, the percentage of lay persons who are under 18 and those in their 40s are approximately equal to the general US population. In contrast to the United Methodist pattern of attracting more mature adults, the very large independent churches draw largely from among people who are under 45.

Note first the 19- to 39-year-old group. Over one-third (35.6 percent) of the population are in this age group, but only a fifth (19.8 percent) of the United Methodist membership. Those are persons in the so-called "baby boom" generation who are currently in their 20s and 30s. The baby boom began in 1946 and ended about 1964. The impact of the high birth rate was reflected in an increase of one-third in the number of infant baptisms and a gain of one-fourth in the enrollment in the children's division of church school. This increase continued until 1955.

Although the baby boom continued until about 1964, the number of infant baptisms began to decrease in 1956. Then in 1960, pastors reported an attendance drop in the children's department and, in the youth and adult departments the next year. That decline in the church school signaled a decrease in the number of lay persons participating in the total life of the congregations. Within a year, worship attendance had decreased, followed by a decline in church membership. Those declines have continued without interruption for more than twenty years.

The declines were strongly influenced by at least two other developments that were also taking place during the decade of the 1960s. First, those years were characterized by turmoil in American society when many established institutions were challenged. Second, almost every mainline denomination was caught up in major restructuring efforts which the leaders hoped would reposition the church for a more effective ministry with those who were caught up in the turmoil. One area severely affected by restructuring was the youth program. The popular Youth Fellowship program of the 1950s was dismantled in favor of other forms of youth ministry. The intention of the planners was to open avenues for youth to become more involved in the total life of the church as full laity. But the results were disappointing. A few young people became more deeply involved in the church, but large numbers of youth simply dropped out of every church activity.

All of the above, plus other well-known sociocultural factors outside the church, have contributed to the current under-representation of many persons who are of the baby boom generation. When compared to mid-size and smaller membership churches, the large membership churches suffered the heaviest losses in the children's and youth departments during the 1960s and 1970s. Those heavier losses are still reflected in the 30-39 and the 40-49 age groups. The shortage may also be due, in part, to the fact that large churches are in urban areas where persons are more likely to be free from family and social expectations of church participation.

At the same time a slightly higher percentage of 19-29-year-olds are in the large membership churches (11.5) than are in the churches generally (8.1). Those data seem to indicate that the younger baby boomers who are now in their 20s prefer larger churches. Many young adults in this age group live in urban areas and some are turning to large membership churches in their quest for meaning and purpose in their lives. They are interested in Bible study and faith development and fellowship. Past denominational ties are secondary in their selection of a church. The primary attractions are a group of like-minded peers, authentic mentors, and a program which meets their perceived needs.

When compared to United States Census data, both large and small churches are over-represented by persons who are above 50 years of age. More than 42.3 percent of the church members are over age 50, compared to one-fourth (26.0 percent) of the US population. An even greater difference is found when the percentage of older adults above 65 who are in our large churches (21.5) is compared with the percentage in the United States population (12.1) who are over 65. Large churches, with their wide-ranging programs, will undoubtedly continue to provide an important ministry to even more persons in that very rapidly increasing group of older adults.

The patterns in the age distribution of the members of large churches are due largely to two factors: community population demographics and deliberate concentration by the churches on particular segments of the population. A large number of persons in the "baby boom" generation are having children. Some refer to this new population wave as the "baby boomlet" generation. Its impact is beginning to be felt in schools and churches. Young parents say they want high-quality education for their children. When a church fills that need, the number of children and young adults who participate regularly in the life of the church can be expected to increase.

There is an increasing tendency among large churches to employ staff with specialized skills to work with particular groups. Programs are targeted and services provided to meet distinct needs. Consequently, in a given community there may be a large church that provides a ministry designed for single young adults. Another may have a program for young marrieds. Another may attract young families providing needed through-the-week daycare for children. Still, another large church may be the place for a high proportion of the high school crowd and their parents. Another may have an effective ministry with older adults. This phenomenon is particularly noticeable in suburban communities and in small to medium-size towns such as county seats. Often the number of persons who are seeking such specialized programs is not large enough to support similar ministries in every local church. Consequently certain larger churches offer them in behalf of all the churches in the community.

Types of Households

Related to age are the types of households found among the members of the large churches. These data are shown in Table II.

TABLE II

*Percent Distribution of Household Types of Large Church Members
by Marital Status*

Single person household	23.8
Couples without children living at home	29.5
One-parent families with children at home	13.3
Two-parent families with children at home	33.4

Note that the figures shown above are for the percentage distributions of households and not for the number of members in a congregation. The 23.8 percent estimate for single person households compares very closely with that of the Census which reports that 22.9 percent of all households consist of one person. It should be remembered that a large percentage of the single person households are widows, which may be one reason for the large number of older church members. Such churches tend to decline unless these older members can be replaced. In contrast, when the percentage of single person households is low, the church is more likely to show membership growth, because there are more families with children who join.

Only a third of the households consist of couples without children living at home. Again, this is because a large number of lay persons are 50 years or more, thus persons whose children are grown. Congregations with a high percentage of couples without children tend to have a relatively stable membership and an above average level of financial support.

When compared to smaller churches, the large membership churches have considerably more one-parent families with children at home. This is due primarily to two factors. First, most large churches are located in urban settings where housing, employment opportunities, and the proximity to services provide a more suitable environment for single parents and their families. Second, large churches usually offer more classes and specialized groups, fellowship opportunities, as well as services and programs which are designed with the needs of single parents in mind. In contrast, many smaller churches are organized around the traditional family unit into which single parents do not as readily fit.

A third of the households in the large church are made up of two parents with children living in the home. A significant finding is that *congregations which are growing report that a large percentage (40.6 percent) of their households consist of two-parent families with children.* The churches with no membership change or with declining membership report that two-parent families with children at home constitute from 24 to 28 percent of their households.

Occupations of Large Church Members

The type and style of ministry of a given congregation are strongly affected by the types of members. Table III shows the percentage distribution of church-related households by the occupation of the principal wage earner.

TABLE III

Occupation of Principal Wage Earner of Large Church Members by Percent

Professional and Executive	25.6
Clerical, Technical, Sales, Middle Management	24.3
Retired	22.4
Blue Collar Employment	12.9
Business Owner	10.9
Farmer/Rancher	2.7
Welfare	1.2

Because large churches are located in urban areas, and often in the major metropolitan centers, the members are employed in urban businesses and industries. Over a fourth are in executive positions or the professions. In contrast, fewer than three members out of one hundred are related to agriculture. Also, only one in eight (12.9 percent) members of large churches are employed in blue collar positions, although there are large numbers of such jobs in urban areas. An extremely small number (1.2 percent) of the members of large United Methodist churches are on welfare.

These data indicate that the majority of those who attend large United Methodist churches come from the middle and upper middle income groups. Other studies have shown that persons from the lower income groups do participate in mid-size and small United Methodist churches. The reasons for this are not fully understood. A number of theories have been suggested but not tested. It is ironic that every predecessor denomination of The United Methodist Church began with a ministry to the poor and disenfranchised. Many small and mid-size churches carry on an effective ministry with and among them. But when United Methodist churches become large, persons with lower incomes appear to go elsewhere. While large churches may not have great numbers of lower income persons who regularly participate in their ongoing programs and activities, many of these churches are deeply committed to a ministry with those who are less fortunate than the majority of their members. That commitment finds expression through strong financial support and hands-on service in a wide variety of programs and activities among inner-city churches and institutions. One large church has entered into a conference-approved, yoked relationship with a small struggling mission church to provide church school teachers, assistance with building maintenance and repair, and other kinds of help that enhance the ministry of the mission.

What Lay Persons Like about the Large Church

Lay persons from large membership churches, like those from smaller ones, list many things they like about their churches. Five characteristics were listed more frequently and given greater importance than others.

The characteristic mentioned most often is the quality of interpersonal relationships that the members have with other persons in the congregation. This is of great importance to lay persons from both large and small churches, and they mention it twice as often as the next desired characteristic. More than three-fourths (76 percent) of the lay persons in large churches list the quality of interpersonal relationships to be of great importance. They use words like *friendliness, caring, loving, supporting, concerned, interested,* and *accepting* to describe what they felt was of the highest importance to them.

In fact, as the size of the church increases, the greater the importance lay persons attach to small groups within the congregation. One independent congregation has 120 groups which meet regularly in homes throughout the metropolitan area. This factor is also associated with an increase in membership. Growing churches provide for more classes and small groups that foster intimate relationships than do churches with a stable or declining membership.

The second characteristic lay persons in large churches like about their church is the variety of ministries and programs that are offered. This factor is not mentioned as frequently by lay persons from mid-size churches and almost never by persons from small membership churches.

Many large churches not only provide more program variety, but they also provide settings in which individuals can be with others with similar characteristics and interests. Examples of this are special classes for those with handicapping conditions, such as hearing, sight, or learning disabilities. Large churches frequently offer services and activities on non-traditional schedules so that persons who must work or have other responsibilities which prevent them from attending the traditional Sunday activities can still participate in certain aspects of the life of the congregation.

The third most frequently mentioned characteristic lay persons like about their church is their pastor. The worship service, and especially preaching, was most frequently mentioned in comments about the pastor. This was followed by pastoral functions such as calling and counseling. The next most frequently mentioned function was the pastor's leadership in the evangelism and outreach ministries of the church. Other functions that were lifted up include teaching the Christian faith and working with the church school teachers and leaders, organizing and administering the business affairs of the church, and directing fund-raising efforts. Pastoral leadership in social reform, connectional services in denomination-related activities beyond the local church, and participation in ecumenical and interdenominational causes were mentioned only occasionally.

Lay persons from mega-churches with 3,000 or more members are inclined to attach more importance to the pastor than do lay persons from smaller congregations. Most of the lay persons from the largest churches listed the pastor either first or second when asked to tell what they like best about their church. Their ranking of the relative importance of pastoral functions is essentially the same as those of lay persons from smaller churches, except they attach more importance to the pastor's symbolic role through which the image and presence of their church is personified.

The fourth most-liked characteristic is music. This is mentioned somewhat less frequently by lay persons from mid-size churches and only occasionally by someone from a small membership church. However, it is not unusual for a lay person from the largest churches to list music before any other characteristic. Such churches do not simply have several choirs; they have a music program. Indeed, the music program is one method for communicating the gospel to a segment of the population.

Most large membership churches employ professional directors or ministers of music and highly skilled organists. They have a large pool of persons from which to recruit talented persons. The quality of music provided by the choirs is sometimes enhanced by employing professional soloists and section leaders. Another factor which enhances the music in many large churches is the quality of the organ. In many communities, persons with musical interests and skills are attracted to a church by the quality or kind of music found there.

The fifth characteristic of large churches which the members considered important but of less importance than the first four was an effective Sunday school. Many lay persons apparently assume that large churches will naturally have good Sunday schools and worship services. However, when the Sunday school does not come up to their expectations, they are quick to report their dissatisfaction. Parents with their children in the Sunday school are most apt to identify the Sunday school as something they like about their church. It is clear that a program to train their children in the faith is of great importance to a significant portion of the members of large churches.

What Members Don't Like

Just as some lay persons are very clear about those things they like about their church, so they are also just as clear about what they don't like and what they think are underlying causes for declining church membership.

The most frequently mentioned source of dissatisfaction is poor preaching. Senior pastors and others serving on the pastoral staff seldom mention the negative effect poor preaching has on the life and ministry of a church. However lay persons are critical of poor or what they feel to be ineffective preaching. About one-third of them believe that poor preaching contributes to church membership decline. An even more startling finding is that almost one-half (43.4 percent) of the administrative board chairpersons who responded to a survey identified poor preaching as a problem area in their church. This underscores the critical importance that lay persons from large membership churches attach to the preaching ministry of their church.

The second most frequently mentioned source of dissatisfaction among lay persons is inadequate programming. Those who are members of large congregations expect their church to offer a variety of programs and services of high quality. Dissatisfaction arises when they feel their church does not offer relevant services and programs, or when those which are offered do not come up to their expectations.

The need for improvements in three program areas was mentioned. First, lay persons say they want their church to provide a greater variety of Sunday school classes and other small face-to-face groups. Second, lay persons say they want more effective evangelism and outreach programs. They are aware of the large numbers of unchurched persons in their communities and the opportunity to minister to these persons. Youth ministry is the third program area that many lay persons identified as a problem area. They are not sure about the kinds of changes that are needed. Nevertheless they feel that what their church is now offering is not effective.

A third source of dissatisfaction is what the members perceive to be a lack of lay involvement. Some of their disappointment grows out of their inability to find avenues of service which they feel are commensurate with their skills and interests. Others mention the tendency of the staff or some other relatively small group of persons to make most of the decisions affecting the life of the church.

The data indicate that lay persons have some definite ideas about what they feel are effective and ineffective characteristics of their church. It can be assumed that their opinions influence their participation.

3. WHAT HAPPENS IN THE LARGE CHURCH?

One characteristic which distinguishes large membership churches from mid-size and small leadership churches is their wide range of programming. In the last chapter, when members of large churches listed what they liked and disliked most about their church, program offerings were second on each list.

The number and variety of program offerings are related to church size. Members of small membership churches tend not to refer to their church's programs when telling what they like about their church. Persons from mid-size churches tend to think of church programs in broad terms, such as children's ministry, youth programs, and evangelistic outreach. As churches increase in size, the program offerings become more varied but also more specific and more sharply focused. Those associated with larger churches think in terms of programs for preschoolers, daycare centers for children of working mothers, youth bell choirs, groups for single parents, and possibly a day school.

The quality and effectiveness of specific church programs are not necessarily related to the membership size of the church. Some small or mid-size congregations offer some programs that members feel are outstanding and most effective. At the same time, some program offerings in the large churches are of such poor quality that members placed them in second place following poor preaching in a list of those things they dislike most about their church. Membership size is a determining factor in the number and variety of programs, but not necessarily a determinant of the quality and effectiveness of specific offerings.

This chapter will focus on three principal program areas—worship, Christian education, and evangelism. Each is an exceedingly important facet of the ministry of every large church; each consists of many elements. These three areas are highly interdependent.

Some Words about Words

First an explanation of language and terminology will be given. The words *program* and *program offerings* are not fully descriptive of everything that goes on in large membership churches. These terms are used because they carry broader connotations and are a bit more comprehensive than others that could be used to describe the broad range of services, activities, and events that make up the total ministry of large churches.

Several different images have been used to describe large congregations with their range and variety of programs. Some have referred to their churches as "full-service" churches. People have become accustomed to full-service banks, full-service supermarkets, and full-service auto repair shops. Others have compared the large church with its multi-faceted program to a large department store which not only supplies the basic needs, but also has or is adjacent to numerous specialty shops that can supply the specific or unusual item being sought. A common description of a large church program is a smorgasbord.

Regardless of the likeness that is portrayed, two implications about large church programming can be drawn. First, not everyone in the congregation is expected to participate in all the programs and activities that are being offered. The programs are designed for persons with specific needs and/or interests. One of the adjustments for some lay persons who move from a small congregation to a larger one is the realization that they must choose in which activities they will participate from those available.

A second implication is that, despite the availability of a range of activities, people can "hide" in a large church and limit their participation to larger gatherings and services. However, persons need to be involved in additional programs, not only for the sake of their own spiritual health but for the health of the church.

The relationship between involvement in church activities and congregational health is illustrated by a senior pastor of an exciting and vibrant congregation who observed:

> We are constantly trying out new programs in order to serve more people, not to get more members. We discover when we are able to really serve people in the name of Christ through a variety of programs, then growth in worship attendance, church membership, and finances follows.

Sunday Morning Worship

Without exception, all indicators point to the Sunday morning worship service as the most critical program offering of large churches. Worship services provide the occasion for the largest number of persons to gather together to hear the Word proclaimed, to celebrate their life together, to examine and deepen their faith and commitments, and to prepare themselves for Christian witness and service.

The worship service is the principal port of entry into the life of the large congregation. It is the focal point of all the ministries and activities of the week. Here persons of all ages and backgrounds come together and share a common experience.

In the minds of an overwhelming majority of worshipers in larger churches, the sermon is the central event in the worship service. A survey of persons who joined a large church during a three-year period indicated that an invitation by a lay person got them to the church for the first time, but the quality of the preaching kept them coming and resulted in their joining. And, the senior pastor is perceived as the functional and symbolic leader of the worship service. He sets the mood and spirit of the worship service. One senior pastor of a rapidly growing large United Methodist church said that when he planned the worship services for his congregation, he tried to "maintain a balance between those elements which would help generate the awe and wonder of a Roman Catholic or Episcopal service and the spontaneity and freedom of a Pentecostal or Baptist service."

Most effective senior pastors believe that they must serve as worship leader and therefore plan and direct the services. Many always open and close the service. Some believe it is important that they make the announcements about the activities and events that are of interest to the whole congregation. The senior pastors of the most rapidly growing churches seldom turn the pulpit over to their associates or to guest preachers. They believe that one of the most important tasks of the senior pastors is that of preaching when the congregation gathers for worship. The lay members concur with this opinion.

A large number of pastors reported that their people want to hear biblically based sermons that will help them get through the week. When preaching, these pastors strive to communicate a relevant and clearly understood message that is delivered in a crisp and exciting style. Humor and nostalgic references are often included. One pastor said, "Everybody likes a little cornbread and milk now and then."

An important second element in the worship service in large churches is the music. Congregations vary considerably in their musical tastes. Some prefer the classical music of Bach and Beethoven, while others prefer some of the contemporary Christian music and old Gospel songs. Some congregations include both. In one congregation the organist and choir use the classics, whereas the congregation sings Gospel songs. Some worshipers appreciate guest soloists and professional section leaders in the choir. Others expect the choir and other musical groups to be made up of persons from the congregation who may or may not have professional abilities. Congregational expectations are often derived from the larger culture and the dominant religious ethos of the community. The music program, however, is one which the congregation perceives to be of high quality and meaningful.

Regardless of the specific kind of music preferred, both pastors and lay persons agree on one point: worship services are enhanced when singable hymns are used. Many pastors report that they always include at least two of the old familiar hymns or Gospel songs in every worship service.

A very important third element in the worship services is the form of worship and liturgy that is followed. Worship service expectations are also strongly affected by the dominant religious culture and background of those who make up the congregation. Churches in the Northern states tend to follow a more formal order of worship, while those in the Southern states tend to be more informal.

As a rule, senior pastors are aware of the liturgical preferences of persons in their congregations and they take them into account when planning the worship service. However, some pastors have not been willing to adjust to the prevailing expectations of the congregation. Others have introduced radical changes in the worship services. In these instances worship attendance has decreased. Some members who have dropped out or attend worship less frequently report that they miss the comfort and stability, which the old familiar elements of the worship service once provided.

There is no doubt that the worship service is central in the life of large membership churches. The importance of a satisfying and meaningful worship service for those in the pew cannot be overemphasized.

Christian Education

A senior pastor said he became convinced of the importance of the Christian education program when a younger mother told him that she and her family started to come to church because their four-year-old son asked her how he could learn about God if she did not take him to church. Because lay persons understand the importance of Christian education, they contribute more time to the many educational activities than to any other program in their church.

Previous research has demonstrated that trends in the church school and other forms of Christian education are the most reliable indicators of subsequent trends elsewhere in the church. These findings were reconfirmed in this study of large churches. There is a very high correlation between the children's division enrollment and the number of persons who are received into membership on confession of faith. The number of adults who are enrolled in the adult department of the church school and in other small study and prayer groups is directly related to a lower church membership dropout rate. In fact, a sizable body of data indicates that as a church becomes larger, so the importance of the church school and other small groups increases. Some pastors indicate that they depend almost entirely on the adult Sunday school classes as the principal means of assimilating new members into the life of the congregation. In several churches, all members are encouraged to spend two hours every Sunday in church. One hour is to be spent in one of the worship services and the other in Sunday school.

Adult and youth Christian education offerings fall into two broad categories—those which are designed to help persons learn about and appropriate different facets of the Christian faith and life, and those which are designed to help persons cope with a wide range of personal and interpersonal needs and concerns. Many Christian educators in large churches try to provide both kinds of instruction on a regular basis.

It is taken for granted that every large church will have a Sunday school with closely graded classes for children, classes and fellowship groups for youth, and several traditional as well as a number of short-term elective learning groups for adults. The large church that does not have such a traditional Christian education program under the direction of a professional Christian educator is a rare exception.

As churches become larger, both the number and variety of Christian education offerings increase. This expansion of the Christian education program permits the development of highly disciplined classes and groups that are sharply focused. One church has an annual Faith Development Academy which regularly involves 200 adults twice a week for a seven-week period. Others regularly employ outside lecturers and instructors with specialized skills and knowledge who provide intensive short-term learning opportunities. Some large churches have recruited a group of instructors who move from class to class to provide instruction in an area of special expertise.

Most large churches also offer Sunday school classes and other study groups that are designed for persons with special interests and needs. One church has several classes for persons with different handicapping conditions. One class is for those who have hearing problems and must communicate in sign language; another class is for the visually impaired; still another is for those who are mentally retarded.

A variety of short-term groups to help persons with particular needs are also found in the large churches. These include such specialized groups as those who have experienced divorce, are coping with grief and loss, managing stress, changing careers, parenting, and caring for aging parents.

Large churches have the resources to utilize the latest technology in the presentation of the gospel. Some are making creative use of audio and video equipment in the Sunday school, including closed circuit TV. The presence of satellite dishes (more often noted at independent and other non-mainline churches) is a further example. This is an area which many large congregations have not yet explored.

Evangelism and Outreach

Some sociologists of religion have likened old established churches, which have declined in recent years, to fossils. The stately churches with beautiful stained glass windows and intricately carved interiors speak eloquently of a glorious past. Many such churches bear the marks of a movement when they were built. Movements are generated when a group of people are caught up in a common venture. But movements tend to eventually lose their momentum, and their energy is redirected to survival efforts. Such is the case with many still large churches that are struggling to regain some of their former vitality.

Other large churches realize their fragility and are constantly working to maintain their momentum through changes in leadership or shifts in the economy or in the communities they serve. Still other churches are on a plateau and have been for some time. They are trying to determine what they must do in order to regain some momentum and how best to maintain that momentum as they experience the new dynamics of a larger congregation.

The solutions to the concerns of those churches and of many others that are concerned about their ministry is directly related to effective programs of evangelism which reach more persons for Christ and the church. A wide variety of effective methods and procedures can be found among churches. We learned that some ways of doing evangelism which were very effective in some churches were a disappointment in others.

There are five pivotal arenas for evangelism in large churches. The first is the point of initial contact with persons. One very rapidly growing metropolitan-type mega-church uses a zone plan to make the initial contact with newcomers to the community. When someone moves into the zone, a member of the church welcomes the newcomer with a basket of fruit, then follows up with a visit a few days later with some helpful information about the neighborhood and the church. Some churches make use of advertising—radio spots, the yellow pages, and direct mail.

A number of plans are utilized to welcome first-time visitors to the church. In almost every instance, the plan provides for some personal recognition of every visitor in the worship service. Some churches provide roving greeters who serve as ushers and make sure that the visitor is introduced to others both before and after the worship service. In almost every instance, an effort is made to get the name, address, and phone number of every visitor. One senior pastor said that he trains his people in the art of greeting visitors and suggests things they might say to them.

A second pivotal arena is the congregational worship service and the climate or atmosphere that is found there. More people who are looking for a church home base their decision on their perception of the friendliness of the people than on any other single factor. Several pastors believe that their people want to be friendly but don't know how to be friendly in church, or they don't know what to say. They include such training in the new member orientation sessions. The pastor of one of the largest churches in America observed that uncaring or unfriendly lay persons have caused more people to withdraw from the church than any other factor.

A third arena is one where persons are helped to make their personal commitment to Christ and the church. This objective sets the church apart from all other groups and institutions. It is the main business of a church, and it is its primary objective. A number of ways are used effectively in large churches to help persons make that commitment. Almost all of them involve Bible study, prayer, personal witness, and instruction.

The most common way for youth is through a confirmation class or a similar learning experience. Since many pastors consider each session to be extremely important, there is a growing tendency to make participation in all sessions a requirement. Confirmation training, or its equivalent, seems to have a residual effect that is lifelong. Adults who continue to be active participants in the church throughout their lifetime are more likely to have had confirmation or catechetical training in their youth than adults who drop out along the way or are just nominally active in the church.

Personal or group counseling sessions are usually provided for adults. Retreats, Bible study and prayer groups, and public worship services also provide settings and occasions for enabling persons to make their commitments to Christ and the church.

A fourth pivotal arena is the assimilation process whereby persons are helped to enter into the faith life of the congregation as active participants in its witness and service. We indicated earlier that, as churches become larger, the assimilation process becomes correspondingly more essential. In most large churches assimilation takes place in small groups. Where congregations have strong Sunday schools, the classes serve that purpose. In other congregations, assimilation is enhanced by relating persons to neighborhood groups, prayer and spiritual development groups, women's or men's organizations, choirs, committees and task forces, or groups that are formed around hobbies or special interests.

The contribution of small groups to evangelism and church growth has been documented by research which has shown that large churches that are growing in worship attendance and membership organized twice as many new Sunday school classes during the preceding five-year period than those which had declined in both membership and attendance.

A fifth pivotal arena is the care of individuals by the congregation. Congregational care is expressed many ways. Some of the most obvious ways are seen in the follow-up plans that are operative in large churches. Some attempt to contact first-time visitors either by phone or a visit within eight hours. Others plan for such contacts within 48 hours. Additional contacts by mail and phone are then made by representatives of different groups and classes in the church for at least a month.

One large rapidly growing United Methodist church has developed an elaborate system for recording the attendance of all members in the weekly worship services as well as participation in other activities. Absence from the worship services for more than two weeks or reduced participation in other activities signals the need for a contact by someone from the church. Several other mega-churches use different variations of what is called an "undershepherd" plan. This method insures regular communication with members of the congregation as well as persons in their neighborhood.

By utilizing this and other plans that are designed for caring, even the largest churches are able to give one-to-one care and support for those who have needs ranging all the way from needing a friend to ease the pangs of loneliness to needing help with a serious physical or spiritual crisis. Some of this type of care is informal and a byproduct of organization in the congregation. A primary value of long-term groups in the

church lies in the interpersonal relationships and informal support sub-
groups that develop. One layman said of another person in his church,
"He's in the people business, and he does it well. He cares."

Other Programs

Much could be written about many more very significant programs
that are found in the large churches in every kind of community. Almost
every effective congregational program was specifically designed and
developed to meet a very real need. Some of the most sterile and ineffective programs are those that some well-intentioned pastor tries because it
worked somewhere else or has been designed by a professional staff
person or a denominational agency and made available to a large number
of vastly different types of churches.

To be effective in any church, and especially the large churches, a
program must be consistent with the overall vision that is shared by the
pastor and the congregation, be developed and led by competent leaders,
and meet a need that is real.

4. THE SENIOR PASTOR

No individual is more important in the development and operation of the large church than is the senior pastor. Many such congregations owe their existence to the leadership of a particular individual. An example is the congregation which today averages just under 3,000 worshipers but which a third of a century ago had closed when the present pastor arrived on the scene. Another United Methodist church which had an average worship attendance of 50 when the present pastor arrived 22 years ago now has over 950 persons attending every Sunday. A Pentecostal congregation has in 19 years grown from 129 members to over 2,900 under the guidance of the same pastor. A seven-year-old independent church has an average weekly attendance of just under 1,800 under the leadership of the pastor who organized the congregation.

While the large independent churches are clearly the result of the leadership of a particular senior pastor, the same phenomenon can be observed in the large churches which are affiliated with the various denominations. Some congregations have become mega-churches since being served by a particular pastor.

This chapter will deal with senior pastors. It will focus on the kind of person who becomes senior pastor of large churches, the characteristics senior pastors have in common, their leadership styles, their role in their denomination, and the problems of succession when they leave.

Characteristics of Senior Pastors

A matter of great interest to both congregations and judicatory officials is the kind of person who makes an effective senior pastor of a large congregation. These pastors are, as would be expected, a rather diverse group of individuals. Nevertheless, they also tend to have certain characteristics in common. These observations are based on interviews with a large number of persons serving as senior pastors of large membership churches. The characteristics are not listed in the order of their importance, but all tend to be found in varying degrees in the senior pastors of the churches studied.

The senior pastor is someone who has a clear sense of who he is and

30

what he is attempting to do. The senior pastor has a strong sense of identity. This is expressed in a clearly articulated theology of the nature and ministry of the Christian church. It is further expressed in the individual's ability to define what the local congregation is attempting to be and to do both in the community and in the larger society. The senior pastor is a leader who knows who he is and where he is attempting to lead the congregation for which he has responsibility.

The senior pastor is an effective preacher. It is impossible to define with any degree of precision just what is good preaching. It is easier to know when one hears good preaching than it is to define it. The styles of these individual pastors vary considerably but all are considered by their congregation and by their peers to be good preachers.

The importance of preaching and the Sunday morning worship service in the large church cannot be overemphasized. This is the activity in which a larger proportion of the members participate than any other. It is through the sermon that the worshiper gains an impression of the faith, attitudes, and personality of the pastor. A pastor must have other skills than simply being an effective oral communicator. However, there are no large membership churches without effective preaching and a meaningful worship service on Sunday morning. Certainly no small churches become large, and no large ones remain so over the long term without a pastor who is an effective preacher and a worship service that is meaningful to the people.

The senior pastors of large churches anchor their ministry in the Bible. Regardless of whether their theological orientation might be classified as liberal, moderate, or conservative, they affirm their reliance on extensive use of the scriptures in their ministries. Some feel that every sermon must be biblically based. Others describe the vitality generated as members of their congregation have met in Sunday school classes and other small groups for Bible study. Some describe the excitement and new insights which grip a congregation when the gospel message is applied to the problems of living in a highly technological society. One senior pastor told how he regularly leads the officers and other key leaders of his congregation through series of intensive Bible studies as they prepare for their annual planning retreat and financial campaign. Another told how he has used the Book of Acts when designing the membership orientation program for new members, and for those who give leadership to the outreach of his church.

References to the critical importance which senior pastors attach to the study and use of the Holy Scriptures as the Word of God was a common theme. They consider the Bible to be the primary source of the motivation and inspiration not only for their preaching but as a factor that informs and shapes other facets of their ministry.

The senior pastor is a person who has a high level of energy. As a group, these individuals are among the hardest working people in Christendom. Their job is the center of their lives and they are thoroughly dedicated to their task. The local church is their main interest. While senior pastors may provide some leadership for the judicatory and the denomination, it is the local congregation which gets their primary attention.

The senior pastor not only works hard but is well organized and thus able to make his efforts produce the maximum results. He does not waste time on unimportant matters but focuses on what is essential to the ministry and the goals of the congregation. He is able to delegate both responsibility and authority to staff and to volunteers for both the program and administration of the congregation.

In order to be able to delegate responsibility the senior pastor must be a good judge of people and their abilities. He is able to select those persons who can perform the variety of tasks necessary for the operation of an effective local church. Not only is he able to select such persons but he is able to persuade them to accept the responsibility for the ministries of the church. One pastor put it this way, "My task is to inspire and motivate people to do the work of the church and to delegate this responsibility to them." He went on to say that the pastor should not attempt to do all the work by himself, but find and enlist laypersons for the tasks.

A senior pastor is able to relate to a large number of persons. He has the ability to remember individual's names. Despite the size of the congregation, the members feel that they know their pastor. To accomplish this, the senior pastor arranges events where he can associate with groups of members so that he can have contact with as many persons as possible.

The senior pastor has the skills to be the chief executive officer of a large organization. This does not mean that he cares for all the details of the church, but rather he enlists professional staff and volunteers to do so. As the chief executive the senior pastor bears the responsibility for the actions of the staff. He gets the accolades when the staff performs well and the blame when they do not. He therefore must be able to give direction to the staff and hold individual members responsible for their performance. The effective senior pastor is a good judge of people and able to recruit staff members who have the skills to perform the needed tasks. He is able to find and employ the right persons for the jobs.

Related to selecting staff and volunteers is the ability of the senior pastor to maintain good working relationships with his staff and among the staff members. To a great degree, he sets the tone for the staff and is the one who must deal with conflict when it arises. The effectiveness of a large church depends on the ability of the senior pastor to recruit, manage, and relate effectively to a staff of professional and volunteer workers.

Finally, the senior pastor must be able to maintain the delicate balance between the remoteness of the role of chief executive officer while maintaining the vital rapport with the large number of church members. He carries the responsibility for the church but must also be a person who cares and is perceived as one who cares about each individual. One senior pastor has all new members and congregational officials to dinner at his home. It is a way for pastor and people to become better acquainted. The long tenure of senior pastors provides more time for pastor and people to know each other. This is an issue in every large church and one which each pastor must work out.

Articulates the Vision

The senior pastor is the person who articulates the vision of and for the congregation. While he helps develop the vision and goals for the church, he is not solely responsible for it. The vision is something which also comes from the people's understanding of the gospel and how it is lived in their personal and collective lives. Nevertheless the senior pastor is the key player in the process. As one man stated, "Every senior pastor knows where he is going and where he wants his church to go."

One senior pastor put it this way, "My task is to develop the faith of the people so that they can reach the unsaved." He went on to explain that the primary task of the pastor was to deal with matters relating to the Christian faith. He said that he had four major responsibilities: first to be the teacher/preacher, second to motivate the people in living the Christian life, third to be an evangelist and win persons to Christ, and fourth to recruit leaders to carry on the work of the church.

The way different pastors state the goals for their congregations will of course vary. The goals themselves will be different depending on the pastor's and congregation's understanding of the nature and purpose of the church. What senior pastors have in common is clarity about the direction they want the church to take and the ability to communicate this effectively to the members.

Tenure

The tendency is for the senior pastor of a large church to remain for a long period of time. Many have served the same congregation for over a decade and several for over a quarter of a century. There are several reasons for long tenure.

The pastors of large churches are committed to the local church and see it as the place of their ministry. They are not looking for "greener pastures" elsewhere but have a long-term commitment to that congregation. Their satisfactions come from being the pastor of a local church.

Many large churches have grown to their present size under the leadership of a particular pastor. When a congregation is growing, the congregation does not want a change of pastors and the pastor himself is reluctant to leave. This results in an attitude by all concerned that is expressed by the phrase, "If it's not broke, don't fix it."

The number of pastors who are able to be senior pastors of large membership churches appears to be limited. It is probably not incorrect to say that most clergy by temperament or training are not particularly well equipped to be the senior pastor of a large church. Therefore, when a congregation gets an effective senior pastor the tendency is to keep him for an indefinite period.

There is some debate over how long a pastor should serve a particular church. Some denominations have a tradition of long-term pastorates; others tend to have the pastors move with some degree of regularity. The United Methodist Church with its itinerant system is one in which most clergy tend to serve from four to eight years in the same church.

Our research indicates that churches tend to become large under the leadership of a particular individual. Congregations in developing communities may increase in membership even when the pastor changes. However, the mega-churches are, in the main, the result of the leadership of a particular pastor. This may be a reason more such churches are independent congregations or in denominations with a call system rather than in a connectional and appointive system of pastoral placement.

The length of time a pastor should remain at a church is one that cannot be mandated, because congregations and pastors vary. Long tenure is said to foster a kind of "personality cult," and at times there is truth in the charge. It is also claimed that four- to eight-year terms make the transition to a new pastor easier than if the departing pastor has served two or three decades. While logical arguments can be made for both long and short terms of service, the fact is that congregations become large under the leadership of a particular pastor. Large churches tend to benefit from longer rather than shorter ministerial tenure.

An Egalitarian Attitude

Related to the difficulty of securing senior pastors is the egalitarian sentiment held by many of the clergy. This is characterized by an attitude that since an individual has been called into the ministry by God, all somehow serve equally. No one pastor is perceived to be performing a service that is more important than any other pastor. An example of the egalitarian emphasis in The United Methodist Church is the discussion of a plan under which all clergy would receive the same salary. The proposals provide for each congregation to be assured an amount based on its ability to pay. The pastors would then be paid from a central office. The amount received by each individual would be a base salary plus certain allowances for such things as family size and years of service. No judicatory has seriously considered adopting an equal salary, but the fact that it comes up from time to time illustrates the egalitarian sentiment.

From a theological perspective clergy are called into the ministry. If the call is genuine, no place of service is less or more important than another. However, it is impossible to provide equality of opportunities and benefits in a judicatory where the individual congregations are of different sizes and have varying amounts of resources. Furthermore, the individuals involved have different levels of energy, ability, and dedication. While all clergy may be performing service of worth, they function differently.

The attitude that pastors should be treated equally can have negative implications for the large church. This is seen in the absence of what organizations call the "fast track," a system whereby persons are given training and experience to prepare them for specific leadership positions. It can be noted in the pressure to limit the search for a senior pastor to the clergy in the judicatory in which the church is located. When a large United Methodist church was assigned a senior pastor from a different part of the country, one pastor complained, "There are a number of men in this annual conference who deserved that church; a person from the outside should not have been brought in."

The large church needs a specific type of pastor. The egalitarian sentiment among the clergy tends to discourage the identification and development of persons to serve such churches. It is critical that all pastors recognize that local churches are different and therefore require leaders with particular skills. The ministry—like other professions—requires a degree of specialization if the church is to serve effectively in our complex society.

Training for Senior Pastors

In light of the important role of the senior pastor in the large church, where and how do persons receive training for that position? Seminaries are not equipped to prepare persons to be senior pastors of large churches. They necessarily place an emphasis on providing students with an understanding of the Christian faith through studies in Bible, theology, and church history. A variety of courses focus on the skills needed for the performance of the ministry in general. These include homiletics, worship and liturgy, pastoral counseling, Christian education, and church administration. There may be courses on the rural or urban church. At this stage of the prospective pastor's training, the work cannot be specialized enough to prepare persons to serve in the different size congregations.

Two tracks are followed by those who eventually become senior pastors of large churches. The most common practice is for the pastor gradually to work his or her way from smaller to larger churches. The pattern is for the seminary graduates to begin their ministry in a small congregation in either a rural community or in a small town. Frequently the individual begins in a multi-church parish which consists of from two to four local churches. If the pastor's performance is satisfactory, he or she expects to move to a larger church which may mean a move from a rural area or small town to an urban center. In due course, a few individuals will receive a call from or be appointed to a large membership congregation.

Training for senior pastors is more acute in The United Methodist Church with its appointive system of assigning pastors than in some other groups. In this denomination the individual is expected to move from smaller to larger churches. The result is that the person who is appointed to a large church after twenty-five years in the ministry may have much to unlearn as well as much to learn.

The question can be raised as to whether this is in fact the best way to prepare persons to serve as senior pastors of large congregations. The experience a pastor receives in serving a small congregation is quite different from that needed to serve a large church. Obviously some skills such as preaching and counseling are similar no matter what size the church membership might be. However small and large churches are very different institutions. The administrative and management skills appropriate in a small church do not necessarily work in the large. The skills necessary to be a pastor of a large congregation and the ability to relate to the various groups within the congregation are different from serving a congregation where a few score persons attend every Sunday.

A second track is followed by some recent seminary graduates and a few other young pastors to the pulpit of a large church. This pattern is more common in denominations that have some form of the call system, and in one area of the country where there are a large number of large United Methodist churches. The would-be large church pastor takes a position as an assistant pastor in a large church. The senior pastor serves as his on-site mentor. The young pastor observes the senior pastor in a number of roles, has opportunities to work with church members in a number of different groups and organizations in the church and community, develops an understanding of what a large church can be and do, and can test and try out his ideas in a real-life situation.

Some of the pastors who take this route have had little contact with small membership churches. They have grown up in a large church; all of their practical experience has been in a large church. They are quite familiar with the dynamics unique to large churches. However, most of them are not ready for their own large church until they have served on the staff of a large church for several years. Consequently, they may serve on the staff of several different churches in order to broaden their experience, to work with several different senior pastor-mentors, and to gain first-hand knowledge of the internal day-to-day operation of more than one large church.

The advantage of this track is that the pastor has not only gained valuable experience but lay leaders of a large church in need of a new senior pastor can check out the individual's track record and demonstrated gifts and graces before negotiations begin.

For example, an independent congregation of over 5,000 is facing the prospect of securing a new senior pastor to replace the present pastor who will soon retire. When asked where they would look for a new pastor, a congregational official replied, "We have first considered the staff here and decided that there was no one who is appropriate. We shall next look at younger senior pastors and staff members of similar churches." This group expects to find someone with experience in a large church.

Pastors of large churches are essentially self-taught. They learn how to manage such congregations by consulting with other pastors in similar situations, by studying other people's successes and failures, by reading relevant material, and finally by trial and error. Frequently they consult experts in other fields whose skills may be useful in helping them manage a large church.

A denomination cannot operate on the assumption that persons who can be effective senior pastors of large churches will somehow rise up. This may not happen unless attention is given to identifying persons who have the potential for the task and to providing them with appropriate training opportunities and experience. Given the importance of the senior pastor, there is nothing the denominations could do that would have a greater positive effect on the large church.

5. THE CHURCH STAFF

The effectiveness of the program of the large church depends to a great degree on the dedication and ability of the staff. While the senior pastor articulates the vision for the congregation and provides overall supervision, it is the staff who give day-to-day and week-to-week direction to what actually goes on in the congregation.

There are two groups of persons who might be considered members of the local church staff. The first are those persons, both ordained and lay, who are employed by the congregation. These persons make up the professional staff. A second group of people without whom no local church could operate are the lay volunteers who do the multitude of tasks necessary for the ministry of the congregation. They could be considered part of the church staff although they tend not to perceive themselves and are not perceived as such. This chapter will focus primarily on the first group or those persons who are employed by the congregation and who carry responsibility for the program of the congregation.

Who Selects the Staff

The church staff is selected by the key leaders of the church with the senior pastor playing a major role. It is frequently the senior pastor who in fact decides whom the congregations will employ. He may have a search committee to advise and work with him; the governing board may ratify the decision which the pastor and the committee makes. Because the senior pastor is responsible for the performance of the staff, it is critical that they be persons with whom he can work and who can work together.

In looking at the selection process of the staff members of the large churches, several common characteristics emerge. First, when congregations are looking for full-time persons, they tend to search broadly for the person with the needed combination of interest and skill. The search is not limited to the immediate area or local judicatory. Congregations are part of both a formal and informal network which they use to locate potential staff. The formal network will be the denominational structure and include the placement offices and judicatory officials. The informal network will consist of pastors and leaders of similar type churches. Such persons come to know each other and may even meet regularly. They informally help a church locate the needed type of staff person.

Second, large churches tend to place more emphasis on competence than on formal credentials. The assumption among many clergy and even lay persons is that seminary training and ordination are desired for professional staff employed by a local church. There are areas of ministry where graduation from a theological school and ordination are absolutely essential. The trend in the past half century has been for the denominations to increase the educational requirements for ordination. The United Methodist Church now has a category of non-ordained professional workers called diaconal ministers, for whom it has been increasing the educational requirements.

The large churches tend to employ staff whom they feel can do the necessary job. The person responsible for the youth program may not have had formal training in that field but has been an effective volunteer youth worker as a lay member of a congregation. Such a person is primarily self-taught and is employed because the senior pastor and other church leaders feel he or she can do the job.

The emphasis on competence and performance also means that the persons who cannot do the job are not retrained. Terminating an employee is not a pleasant task and it can be particularly hard for a church. Nevertheless, mistakes are made. The large church generally will not continue a staff member who is unable to perform adequately.

Staff Tenure

Large churches tend to retain capable staff members for long periods of time. It is not uncommon to encounter persons who have served on the staff of the same church for over a decade or even for more than twenty years. The practice is for the congregation to find persons who can perform the necessary tasks and to keep them indefinitely. The churches also provide adequate compensation for the staff so that the individuals do not feel that they are underpaid or exploited. As one pastor to youth in a congregation of over 5,000 members put it, "The staff here is well paid so that no one finds it necessary to look for another job to make ends meet." This church tends to retain staff.

Although the level of salary is important, that alone will not attract and retain a good staff. The individuals must feel that they are doing something worthwhile and that they are appreciated by both the congregation and the senior pastor. The staff member must sense that his or her service is an expression of the call to that particular form of ministry.

One senior pastor commented that his goal was to secure staff who were specialists and to provide ways for them to keep abreast of their field. He said this had proved to be an effective method of keeping a good staff. Another man stated, "It is important that the senior pastor not be a threat to the staff. I'm success-oriented and I expect my staff to be success-oriented. You should not, however, compete with your staff. The only record I want to break is my own."

The consensus of the senior pastors and lay leaders of the large churches is that the staff should be competent specialists. Appropriate efforts should be made to retain those persons who are doing a good job while less than adequate performance should not be tolerated.

Staff Relationships

Working on the staff of a church means rather intense relationships both with members of the congregation and with colleagues. Even large churches have a relatively small number of employees when compared with various other institutions. The members of a church staff tend to see a lot of each other. When combined with the nature of the issues and problems with which they deal, numerous opportunities for conflict are provided.

The person who sets the tone and the style for the way the staff works together is the senior pastor. Someone must be in charge. This does not mean that the senior pastor is arbitrary but it is with him that "the buck stops." A large church cannot be effective if an attempt is made to have the staff function as administratively equal.

Clarity of each individual's area of responsibility is a major method of insuring good staff relations. The entire staff and the lay members must understand what each person is expected to do and not do. Such clarity does not prevent a collegial relationship. It may enhance cooperation. One senior pastor reported that while each member had a part of the church program for which he/she was responsible, it was understood that staff and laity would assist each other as needed. He said, "The staff members understand that they can call on each other to assist in the various programs and they do so. We work out the details in our regular staff meetings."

The relationship of the members of the staff to the governing board of the large church is a matter which is handled in different ways. This ranges from the staff members being responsible only to the senior pastor to each individual reporting directly to the board. In one congregation with a staff of five clergy, only the senior pastor actually met with the board. The other pastors were not expected to attend board meetings unless there was an item on the agenda involving their area of responsibility, in which case they were invited. One member said, "We have an annual evaluation by the board but will not attend more than a couple of other meetings of that group during the year."

The United Methodist Discipline requires that each church have a Pastor-Parish Relations Committee which is to counsel with the pastor and members of the staff regarding a variety of matters, including relationships between the pastor/staff and the congregation, priorities in the use of time, compensation, housing, and other practical matters. Not only the pastor but all members of the staff, both lay and clergy, are expected to have access to the Pastor-Parish Relations Committee.

It is impossible to say that one method is better than another in every instance. And the effectiveness of the staff and their ability to work together always depend on the persons involved in a particular church. Our observation is that working relationships are better and the ministry of the local church more effective if the responsibilities of each member are clear and the senior pastor is clearly in charge and able and willing to supervise the work of his associates.

The Assistant Pastor

The staff members who as a group appear to be less satisfied with their positions are the ordained assistant/associate pastors. In fact, some of the most unhappy staff members are United Methodist assistant pastors. This is a more serious problem among United Methodists that in any other denomination.

There are two general types of assistant pastors. The first tend to be recent seminary graduates who are beginning their careers as members of the staff of a large church. These persons see this experience as a continuation of their seminary training, a kind of extended internship. It is an opportunity to gain experience in a large congregation and to work under the direction of an experienced senior pastor. These assistants do not plan to spend their careers as members of the staff but expect to move after two or three years to become pastors of their own churches. One senior pastor made an agreement with each of his associates that they would stay for a three-year term but no longer. He was careful to give them responsibilities which would assure a variety of experiences. The assistant pastors left at the end of the three years with the feeling that they had learned a great deal and were better prepared to serve a church of their own. As would be expected, this group of short-term assistant pastors are likely to be satisfied with their position.

A second group of persons are on the staff of a large church for secondary reasons, not because they prefer the position. Being an associate pastor enables them to meet a personal or family need. They may find the associate's position less objectional than an alternative. For example, an assistant pastor of a large urban church accepted the position because his wife wanted to complete a graduate degree in a nearby university. He did not like being a member of a staff and would have preferred to be the pastor of his own smaller congregation. He was unhappy, and the senior pastor and congregation were dissatisfied with his performance.

A pastor accepted a parish of two churches in a rural area upon graduation from seminary. He had grown up in a large city and didn't like living in the small town where one of his churches was located. To get back into the city, he accepted a call to be an assistant pastor at a large downtown church. While he was happy to be living in the city, he also enjoyed preaching and resented the fact that he was able to preach only a few times each year on the Sundays when the senior pastor was away.

There is, of course, a group of clergy whose interest and personality seem to equip them for being a general assistant/associate pastor. They do not want to be a pastor-in-charge or to preach regularly. The number of such persons seems to be limited.

A problem is that being an assistant/associate pastor tends not to be considered a vocation. Persons who feel that they have been called to the ministry or to be ministers of Christian education or to the ministry of music may plan to spend their lives in that field. Few persons seem to feel that they have been called to be a permanent assistant.

A related problem is that there is no clear career pattern for an assistant pastor. The successful pastor may anticipate moving to larger churches with increased responsibilities. He or she and other clergy have an understanding of what constitutes success and results in upward mobility. This is not true for the associate pastor who already is on the staff of a large church. To move to another large church is not necessarily perceived as an improvement for the individual. The general assistant pastor who wishes to remain in that type position is perceived as being locked in the same type of job indefinitely.

Another factor is the lack of job definition for the general assistant pastor who may feel that he or she is assigned the tasks that the senior pastor does not wish to do. In some cases this may be true, but even when the assistant is given specific areas of responsibility, he or she is always perceived to be (and in fact is) subordinate to the senior pastor. Lay persons tend not to give equal status to the assistant and the senior pastor. For example, a visit from the assistant is considered by many laypersons as not being quite equal to a visit from the senior pastor.

The role of the assistant pastor changes as the church becomes larger. Among the churches with approximately 1000 to 2000 members, the assistant pastor usually carries responsibility for several program areas, such as Christian education, evangelism, and missions, or for one or two of the age group ministries. There is a growing tendency in some churches of this size for the assistant pastor to be called the Minister of Program. When this occurs, he or she still has primary responsibility for one or two program areas and/or one or more age groups, but also gives supervision to almost all of the programs except worship. The areas over which he or she has general supervision are often staffed by other staff persons, either on a full-time or part-time basis or by volunteers.

As the congregation approaches and moves beyond 2000 members, the assistant pastor's role may take one of two directions. First he or she may be given additional administrative and supervisory responsibilities. More of the hands-on responsibility for day-to-day programming is increasingly assumed by other staff persons who are brought in for more specialized tasks, such as ministry with children, ministry with youth, or outreach or congregational care ministries.

The second direction that the assistant pastor's role may take, as congregations become larger, is that of assisting the senior pastor with the range of pastoral duties such as pastoral calls, funerals, weddings, and counseling. When the assistant pastor's role moves in this direction, he or she is frequently called an Associate Pastor.

Some of the most effective pastors of large churches have solved what they call the problem of the general assistant pastor by not having one. They will, of course, supervise a large staff, but each member has been employed to work in a defined area. One person may be minister to youth, another may be minister of evangelism, a third may be an administrator with responsibility for the physical plant, while another will make pastoral visits. Each person can work in his or her area of interest and expertise. While the staff members may preach on appropriate occasions, there is no question as to who has responsibility for the Sunday morning worship service. One senior pastor has assigned certain services to members of his staff. One person has primary responsibility for the Sunday evening service, while another is in charge of the Wednesday evening service. This gives the staff members an opportunity to preach or teach regularly, while avoiding competition over who will preach on Sunday morning.

There is probably no group of persons whose responsibilities and relationships are more varied from church to church than full-time staff persons in the larger churches who specialize in specific areas of programming. Their job descriptions may range all the way from minister to the shut-ins, to coordinator of volunteers; from director of the daycare center to the minister of music; or from minister to singles to director of recreation.

For the most part, each of them has been brought onto the staff because the senior pastor and other leaders in the congregation became aware of an unmet area of ministry. Often the need arises out of the particular community in which the church serves. Sometimes, a congregation may become aware of a segment of the population who are not being served by any church. Changes in age distribution within the congregation, or a decision to develop new or expanded forms of ministry, may also dictate the need for additional staff leadership.

Church Business Administrators

The rapid expansion of through-the-week church programming and activities which began in the late 1940s generated the need for a new kind of staff person to manage the business affairs of the church. Thus emerged the church business administrator. Today most churches with an average worship attendance of about 500 or more have added a church business administrator or manager to the staff. They have assumed many of the essential and time-consuming administrative responsibilities that were previously carried by the senior pastor and other program staff members.

While the specific responsibilities may vary with each church and its program, almost every church business administrator performs several basic functions. Foremost among them are tasks related to the management and interpretation of the church's finances. These include such tasks as preparing budgets, managing payrolls, keeping up with tax changes and insurance needs, and making purchases. Most church business administrators carry responsibility for the maintenance of buildings and equipment and the supervision of maintenance workers, volunteers, and kitchen and dining room personnel. They are usually responsible for scheduling the use of church facilities and equipment. A very important responsibility is that of dealing with salespersons, vendors, and persons in need of assistance.

They are to the management of the business affairs of the church what the associate pastor is to the program ministry of the church. Because of this very important role in the life of the church, most church business administrators are directly accountable to the senior pastor.

Part-Time Staff

There is a trend in the increasing number of part-time staff members in large churches. A variety of persons with a wide range of backgrounds are being employed. Some are members of the congregations who began as volunteers and gave such valuable service that they were added to the staff. Some are persons with theological training but who want to work only part-time. Included in this group are women who hold degrees from a theological seminary and are now married. Some have children and are unable or do not wish to be employed full-time. Others cannot move to a place where they might secure a full-time position because their spouse is unwilling or unable to relocate. Given the growing number of women seminary graduates, it is likely that there will be an increasing supply of part-time (male and female) persons with professional training available for staff positions in the period ahead.

Churches are also securing persons as part-time staff with a wide variety of backgrounds and training. There is an increasing number of college trained persons who are available to serve in large churches. One congregation employed a man as youth worker who was a popular disk-jockey at a local radio station. Another had a high school teacher as a director of children's work. Congregations of all sizes have long employed part-time organists and choir directors. It is not surprising that large churches should continue the practice in other program areas.

There are several reasons for the increase in the number of part-time staff. The first is economic. It costs less to employ persons part-time than it does full-time. This is especially true if the full-time person is ordained, which requires that the congregation provide housing and various other benefits specified by the denomination. Local church leaders tend to feel that they receive good service from a part-time staff for less cost.

A second factor in the increasing number of part-time staff is the desire on the part of the local church to have complete control over who is employed. If an ordained person is desired, the congregation not only has to meet the denomination's requirements, but it may not have the final say in who is selected for the position. The individual under consideration may need to be approved by a denominational authority or, in the case of The United Methodist Church, every ordained minister must be appointed by the resident bishop who has the final authority in saying where every ordained minister shall serve. By employing lay and part-time people, the local congregation retains complete control over who shall be on the staff.

6. MANAGING THE LARGE CHURCH

In *Rekindling the Flame,* the authors observe that the Book of Acts is essentially an account of the way the apostles functioned as they guided the very fragile community of believers through the first turbulent years. They contend that the church has always needed both leaders and managers in order to maintain its vitality and strength. They express a concern about the predominance of managers and the scarcity of leaders in the policy- and decision-making bodies of the contemporary church. At the same time, the dominance of leadership characteristics found in local church pastors is affirmed.

The distinctions between leaders and managers are essentially those which organizational developmentalists use to describe the differences between transformational leaders and transactional leaders. Leaders have a vision of the goals that can be achieved, are able to communicate the vision, and are able to motivate others to join in the struggles to bring about the changes that are essential in order to achieve the goals. Managers work within the organizational culture to provide the stability and maintain the values that have been achieved. They know what needs to be done and how to do it. Elsewhere in this book we have emphasized the leadership functions on some of the management issues that are integral to the operation of large membership churches.

Management and Membership Size

The management process in a local church is strongly influenced by the size of the congregation. The management decisions of very small churches tend to be made by the members as a whole or by one or two recognized leaders. The process of decision making is informal. In many rural communities the people (frequently the men) often settle matters while standing in the church yard during the break between Sunday school and the worship service. Decisions also might be made during the Sunday school assembly under the leadership of the Sunday school superintendent.

When the church is part of a multi-church parish, the pastor's input may be minimal. One pastor who was serving four rural congregations preached in each church every other Sunday. When he arrived one week to conduct the worship service, he was surprised to discover that the building had been painted inside and out and new carpet had been installed in the sanctuary. He had not been aware that the members were even considering redecorating the church.

The larger the congregation, the more formal and the more complex the management process becomes. A large church cannot operate on the principle of participatory democracy. Someone must have the authority to make policy, set the budget, and employ the staff. In most churches the authority for management decisions resides in a governing board. Responsibility for giving direction and oversight and allocating funds for the numerous programs, services, and activities are lodged in various organizations, committees, and task forces. The ongoing day-to-day functions of the church are supervised and managed by the senior pastor and members of the employed and volunteer staff.

The way in which those management responsibilities are carried out greatly affects the total ministry of every church. Good management is unobtrusive; it is not obvious until it is lacking. Then, like a piece of machinery which lacks grease, it begins to squeak and grind and may eventually cease to function. The complexity of managing large churches increases with their membership size. So does the need for skillful management.

Skilled managers are needed to raise the funds for large annual budgets; to build and maintain extensive physical facilities; to recruit, train, and direct a constantly changing professional and volunteer staff; to establish and cultivate linkages with other institutions and churches in the community. Other management needs could be added to the list.

Will the Real Managers Please Stand Up?

A term which has traditionally been used in The United Methodist Church and its predecessor denominations is *pastor in charge*. Equivalent terms are used in most other denominations. One of three major assignments given to the pastor in charge by the *Book of Discipline* is that of "administering the temporal affairs of the congregation" (Par. 438). The pastor is also given the responsibility "to be the administrative officer of the local church and to assure that the organizational concerns of the congregation are adequately provided for" (Par. 441). There is no question about the pastor's assigned responsibility to be the primary manager of every United Methodist local church. That assignment comes with the same authority and force as do the responsibilities for preaching the Word, administering the sacraments, providing pastoral care, and performing other assigned functions.

The responsibility for managing the affairs of large membership churches poses serious problems for many senior pastors. They have become pastors of large churches because they do have a vision of what the church can and should be. They are able communicators and interpreters of that vision, and they have the ability to motivate their members to join them in pursuit of that vision. But they may have only moderate interest in managing the affairs of the church. Some senior pastors say they are very frustrated by the heavy administrative demands placed on them. Like most clergy, they have received very little formal training in management. As churches become larger, budgets increase, and staff and personnel matters become more complex and critical. More organizations are established to provide for expanding ministries; more stress is placed on physical facilities. The demands on the senior pastor's time and energy seem never-ending.

A United Methodist pastor's comments were representative of a number of others. He reported that, several years ago when he was having another sleepless night, he realized that he and others in the church had reached an impasse. He went on to say that just because they were the largest church in the area, they thought they should try to do everything.

> My blood pressure had soared and my doctor told me I would have to slow down. Members of our staff were complaining that they were being run ragged. We were always having meetings that never got anywhere. Several of our finest lay persons were showing signs of burnout. We never seemed to be able to catch up with our budgetary needs. It seemed that we were spinning our wheels and we were trying to go in all directions at the same time but were just getting more mired down and frustrated. We just had to make some changes.

He recounted how he and a few trusted friends decided on a plan that eventually brought some order out of the gathering chaos. Other pastors reported similar experiences. Effectively managed large churches have certain characteristics in common. What follows is a composite summary of some of the most effective church management ideas that senior pastors shared with us.

Some Ideas That Have Worked

The beginning point for all church management efforts is to clearly define the central purpose and nature of the ministry of the church. To put it another way, it is very important that the senior pastor and key leaders of the church be clear about their overall vision of their church and its ministry to their members, in the community and in the world. These pastors struggled to discover what God was calling the church to be and to look like now and in five or ten or twenty years from now. Some senior pastors named a group of well-informed laypersons to work with them in the development of a statement of purpose; others preferred to work with members of the staff; and some preferred to work alone before testing their vision with others.

The second phase was sharing the statement and having it adopted. Arrangements were made to have all persons concerned examine and study it. Some persons offered suggestions; others raised questions. It was essential that a common understanding of the vision and a shared commitment to it be achieved. Such a commitment to a common vision was found in almost every vital large church that we studied.

To simply adopt a carefully crafted statement of purpose is not enough. Many good statements of purpose have not been effective because nothing ever resulted from them. In order for the vision to become a reality, the statement of purpose must reflect the vision and must be translated into viable programs, services, and activities. Ideally, everything a congregation does or plans to do is shaped and evaluated in light of what it can contribute to the realization of its stated purpose.

The task of translating a purpose statement into ministry is the third step. This is not unique to the large church. However it is usually much more complex in the large church because these congregations have a multifaceted ministry. Pastors have approached the task in different ways. Some have worked with the staff; others have named a small task force; still others have enlisted the governing board. Some have asked every organization and committee in the church to do their planning in light of the purpose statement, and one pastor invited each of the neighborhood groups in the congregation to study the purpose statement and use it as a guide for their activities.

Regardless of the method that is used, most procedures begin by identifying the large areas or niches through which the congregation carries on its work. When combined, they comprise the total ministry of the congregation. These usually include such broad areas as age-level and family life concerns, Christian education and the Sunday school, Bible study and spiritual formation, evangelism and community outreach, and stewardship and finance. These are then examined in light of the needs of the people, both those in the congregation and those not being served or reached by the church. Attention is then given to the specific programs, services, and activities that are currently being offered within each broad area; those that are needed are identified. Next, professional and volunteer staff services in each area are examined and any desired changes in personnel and skill needs are noted. Space needs are determined and the adequacy of current physical facilities is reviewed and needs are noted. An analysis is then made of the strength and scope of the church's financial base, and future budgetary needs are projected. In most instances, it is at this stage in the process that the findings are coordinated and presented to the governing board for their consideration and appropriate action.

A fourth phase in the management process is that of setting priorities. Priorities for churches means deciding what will be done and what will not be done at a given time. The needs which the church might address are virtually infinite. To decide how the congregation's resources of people and funds will be used is always difficult.

Priorities are of two kinds which are closely interrelated. First, some priorities should be established on the basis of the relative immediate importance of the various areas of ministry to the total ministry of the church. For example, an influx of young families into the community may indicate a need to give high priority to the family life program and the establishment of a daycare center.

Second, time priorities should be set. A timeline is a useful tool for setting time priorities. For example, it is always advisable to recruit and train leaders before launching a new program or offering a new service.

One senior pastor reported that, in his church, plans were made in five-year segments. One major area of ministry was selected and emphasized over all the others for one entire year during the five-year period. One year additional energies and support were given to an expansion of their family ministry programs and services; another year the congregation concentrated on stewardship and broadening their financial support base; in another year the emphasis was on evangelism and church growth. Foreign missions were targeted in another year. The pastor said continual special attention is given to each emphasis for four or five years after the special emphasis. He has found that it takes about that long to ensure continued vitality and strength in the ministry area.

Another senior pastor, who also follows a five-year plan, reported that special attention is given to designated programs and services on a quarterly basis. Prior to beginning the special emphasis, persons are recruited who will focus their energies in the designated area of ministry, and they are given training for their task. The special emphasis is then launched with an intensive Bible study and understood course of action.

A fifth and very important step in the church management process is the assignment of responsibilities to staff and other leaders. A factor that should be remembered is that our basic leadership and management styles are integral to our personalities. It is very difficult or impossible for many of us to change those styles or to develop the high level of competency that is required in every area. The wise senior pastor will assume direct responsibility for administering programs and services in which he has competence. However, he will not hesitate to delegate responsibilities to someone else who has demonstrated his or her management skills in those areas. A senior pastor of a well-managed large church said he knows that his greatest gifts are not in administration and management. Consequently, when he came to his present church he arranged to bring on to the staff a highly skilled business manager and an associate pastor with proven program planning and administration ability. Another senior pastor has limited his relationship to committees related to worship, finances, the nomination of lay officials, trustees, communication, and staff parish relationships. Still another senior pastor gives his personal attention to the committee on evangelism, long-range planning, and finances, and to an ongoing training program for local church officers.

Pastors of large churches discover that it is absolutely necessary to delegate a number of management responsibilities to employed and volunteer staff persons and to designated lay officers. One pastor said that if he was personally involved in everything that went on in his church, there was not enough going on. One senior pastor whose church is involved in a multi-million dollar building project said that the project will be carried through to completion by a committee which is made up of very capable lay persons.

Senior pastors say that the keys to the successful delegation of church management tasks are to know which responsibilities to keep and which to delegate and to whom to delegate them. Successful delegation is enhanced by three factors: comprehensive job descriptions which have been mutually agreed upon by all concerned; a plan for regularly reviewing and evaluating the performance of church management tasks; and a system of accountability.

The Governing Board

Although the senior pastor is the chief administrative officer in most large churches, he and the congregation need a governing board. Policies must be set, budgets must be drawn up and managed, and provisions must be made for employing, staffing, and maintaining physical facilities.

A common factor in many large churches is a small, but powerful, governing board. Only a few persons are involved in making the policy and administrative decisions. Authority is given to a relatively few persons who take their responsibility with great seriousness. In one large church with just under 3,000 members the board consists of seven men. Each member agrees to serve for a period of six years but may not serve more than one consecutive term. While serving on the board, persons may not hold another office.

An independent church with a membership of over 6,000 is governed by a board of fourteen persons. This congregation also operates a day school with more than 900 students in grades kindergarten through twelve. A subcommittee consisting of the senior pastor and three board members is responsible for the day school.

The pastors and lay leaders of some very large congregations believe that a small governing board is both an efficient way of managing the church and an effective means of carrying out the ministry of the congregation. When one pastor was asked about the denominations from which persons transferred their membership to his church, he replied that the largest number had been Baptists, followed by Methodists and then Roman Catholics. When asked why Baptists might want to join his church, he replied, "We do not have a lot of business type meetings; we almost never have a congregational meeting for business purposes. Our people are engaged in ministry." That congregation has a board of seven lay persons with the pastor serving as the chairman.

The question may be raised as to whether or not this is the best or even proper way to manage a local church. It should be noted that lay persons are not excluded from participation in a vast array of programs and services. A concerted effort is made to provide ways for lay members to engage in ministries. There are many committees and task forces which provide opportunity for a variety of lay participation. The interested member in one church may serve in a variety of ways, such as assisting persons in the parking lot, staffing the information booth, teaching Sunday school, telephoning shut-ins, or working in the shelter for the homeless. Authority for managing the affairs of this church is delegated to the senior pastor and the governing board.

When the board is small and has great authority, board members must not only possess the appropriate skills but must also have the confidence of the members of the congregation. One senior pastor of a mega-church said that he never asked a lay person to assume a major position in the church if the church job was the biggest thing in that person's life. He went on to say that he wanted his top leaders to have demonstrated leadership ability in other positions.

In The United Methodist Church, as in several other denominations, the membership of the Administrative Board is made up of designated staff members and the chief officer or a representative of each of the principal organizations, councils, and committees of the congregation. The officers of the Administrative Board are elected annually. The senior pastor serves as the administrative officer for the board.

In many large United Methodist churches, the Administrative Board has a hundred members or more. Because the board is so large, most of the actual work of the board is done in subcommittees named by the Administrative Board or in one of the other organizations or committees represented in the membership of the board. The basic function of most Administrative Boards in large churches is that of receiving and acting on reports that were generated in one of the many smaller program or administrative units in the congregation. While provisions are made to insure the practice of participatory democracy, in actual practice most of the initial planning and decision making in the large United Methodist churches is done by smaller groups of persons. The governing board has the authority to approve or disapprove all matters that are brought before it, but due to the size of the board and the number of items that are often on the crowded agenda, discussion and debate tend to be limited. Consequently, Administrative Boards sometimes take actions on matters that do not represent the best thought of the governing board members or of the staff.

An exceedingly important factor is the relationship of the senior pastor to the governing board. In large churches with small boards, the pastor is highly influential, if not dominant. This is especially true in those churches where the current pastor was also the founding pastor. In churches with large governing boards, such as in The United Methodist Church, the senior pastor is designated as the administrative officer. However, his influence in some instances may be limited and even overridden by the lay persons who make up the membership of the governing board. On the other hand, when the members of the Administrative Board and the senior pastor concur, the actions of the board have a broad base of support throughout the congregation.

The administrative styles of pastors and local churches vary. In the large membership church the policy decisions tend to be made by a relatively small board. The staff and volunteer leaders carry out the policies set by the board. Opportunities are provided for the members to participate in a vast array of programs and service ministries. Small groups provide the intimate fellowship for the members. This complex organization which is the large church in a variety of ways proclaims the message of the gospel and serves in the name of Christ.

7. LOCATION AND BUILDING

The location of a church and the facilities which it provides continue as extremely important factors in determining who attends and what types of activities are provided. The importance of a good location has changed since the times when churches were built in the center of rural villages or placed in urban neighborhoods so most members could walk to church. And while buildings are constructed to house programs, the building itself will lend itself to certain kinds of activities and restrict others. Furthermore, the building makes a statement about what the congregation is and does to all who pass by; it tells something about who the people are and what happens there. In this chapter we shall consider how the location and the building affect the large church.

The Importance of Location

A church is a group of people who share a common faith and who meet regularly to worship, to learn about the faith, and to minister in a variety of ways to each other and to non-members. From time to time, every pastor has asserted that the church is not the building but the people of God. While this is correct, it is also obvious that the people must assemble in a particular place. Where a church is located will, to some degree determine, who will attend.

A church tends to be located where it is convenient for the members. The people have to be able to get to the church without spending an undue amount of time or effort. After all, the members are not only expected to be present on Sunday mornings but at various other times during the week for a variety of activities. At one time the large churches were in the center of the city because that was the place most accessible to large numbers of people. The public transportation system brought people downtown. The now almost universal use of the private automobile has changed this. In many cities it has become inconvenient to drive downtown and difficult to find adequate parking facilities. The outlying shopping mall has replaced the central business district as the place where people make many of their retail purchases. The shopping center, surrounded by its vast expanse of parking lot, now is where a large proportion of Americans go to shop, eat, and take in a movie. The mall is the Main Street for the contemporary generation. It is where teenagers go to "hang out." The shopping center is entirely a commercial enterprise. While there are occasional civic activities such as performances by choirs during Christmas or a display of elementary school pupils' art, there are no nonprofit permanent institutions. The public library must be in a less expensive location as must the churches.

The change in patterns of transportation means persons coming to church will come by car. This has resulted in several factors which make a particular location desirable for a church. The first is accessibility. It must be possible for the individual to drive to the church and get in and out of the parking lot without undue difficulty or hazard. A location on a major street is an advantage. The church should be easy to find. One tucked away in the middle of a quiet residential neighborhood will have difficulty attracting people because it is difficult to locate.

A second factor is visibility. A church which can be seen by a great number of people as they pass by has an advantage over one that is hard to find. Individuals probably are more likely to select a church if they can find it easily. Signs help but are a poor substitute for a visible location.

A third factor is adequacy of the site. With people coming by car, adequate parking is an absolute necessity. The loyal member may put up with a great deal of inconvenience, parking a block or two away if necessary. The potential member who has not yet developed ties to the congregation may be less willing to put up with inconvenience. Every large church has adequate parking.

Virtually every church location is the result of compromise and, hence, less than perfect. The most desirable site may not be available or available only at a cost that is prohibitive. The visible location may have fewer parking spaces than needed. The choice which will maximize the desirable qualities is the one which must be made.

It must be remembered that, while a poor location can place a congregation under a serious handicap, the best location will not guarantee success. Location can be an asset to be exploited or a handicap to be overcome. Some effective churches have been developed at poor locations, while there have been failures at excellent sites. In the final analysis, the individual tends to select a church because of such factors as the kind of people who make up the congregation and what happens there. Location is very important but it is not the sole criterion by which the choice is made.

The Church Building

Every church building serves two purposes. The first is functional: A building provides space where the various activities can take place. There is one type of space designed for worship and another for education. Still other facilities are for recreation and fellowship. Some parts of the building are for activities which are supportive of the other functions. The choir room provides a place for the choir to prepare for participation in the worship service; the kitchen is supportive of fellowship activities. This first purpose can be best expressed in the statement that the function of a church building is to house programs.

The second purpose is symbolic. The building explicitly and implicitly incorporates certain symbols which represent aspects of the faith and beliefs of the people and the tradition and culture of the denomination. The type of steeple on an Eastern Orthodox church clearly identifies its denomination. Red doors make a statement about the worship service. The symbols and figures in the stained glass windows depict the beliefs and significant events in the members' understanding of the development of their faith. The circuit rider featured in many United Methodist churches is a symbol of that denomination's early history and its system of an itinerant ministry. The cross atop the steeple indicates that the structure houses a Christian congregation.

The two purposes are combined in every church building which must provide space for a variety of activities while incorporating appropriate symbols. A particular facility will reflect not only the theological understandings of the congregation but certain sociological and economic factors. The style of a building and the elaborateness of its furnishings will, to some degree, reflect the level of affluence of the congregation and the people's understanding of the Christian faith. Thus, a particular church will reflect the standards and expectations of the people who worship there.

Flexibility

A congregation is a dynamic ever-changing entity. It may be growing or it may be declining in size. Even if it is remaining about the same size, members still come and go. At one time there may be a high proportion of young families with school-age children. At another there may be a group of people who have grown older together and thus a large proportion of senior citizens. A continual problem for churches is that buildings constructed to serve one group of members are not appropriate for another. The once large urban church now has unused classrooms which were bulging with children a generation ago but which are not needed by the now older congregation.

While every church may have some problem with the flexibility of its space, the large congregation finds this much less so than do smaller churches. The large church will tend to have a range of facilities which were designed to provide space for a variety of programs. Nevertheless, even large congregations change as a result of different space requirements. It is important that buildings be designed for the maximum flexibility so that they can be used for whatever is needed in the present and may be needed in the future.

The Message of the Building

The church building conveys a message to those who pass by and those who consider entering. This message can be one which welcomes people or gives a signal that the congregation has a tendency toward inclusiveness. A building tells something about the people who make up the congregation. Over the door most visible from the parking lot one large church has in letters a foot high: "VISITORS' ENTRANCE." No person attending for the first time could miss that sign. Inside are volunteers to welcome newcomers and direct them to the sanctuary or the appropriate Sunday school class. Another church has parking lot ushers who will help you find a space and provide an umbrella if it is raining.

Another large church has several parking spaces convenient to the entrance labeled "Reserved for Visitors." The message of welcome is clearly communicated to anyone who might attend. The senior pastor of another large and rapidly growing congregation will not permit a reserved parking space for himself or the other members of the staff. He insists that the staff park at the far edge of the lot. He says that the spaces nearest the building "be saved for the worshipers." This attitude seems to be held by a minority of congregations. Most have the parking spaces near the entrance labeled "Reserved for Staff" which communicates a different message to the newcomer.

In visiting the large congregations, one notes that care is given to seeing that the facilities are attractively maintained. The grass is cut and the shrubbery trimmed. The building is clean and neat. Last quarter's church school literature is not stacked in the corner of the classroom.

This may be due to the fact that the congregation is large enough to employ staff to do much of the necessary work. Whatever the reason, it is obvious that some persons are giving thought to the physical facilities and what message the building conveys to people. Attention is given to helping people find their way in a large and complex facility. Signs are prominent and the directions clear. An information table may be staffed on Sunday mornings. This is necessary in a large church, but it also is one of the reasons the congregation has grown to its present size.

To the regular attenders, the church building is familiar territory. They know their way around; it is like being at home. When one is familiar with a facility, it is normal to overlook its assets and liabilities. A helpful exercise for both clergy and laity of any size congregation is to visit a strange church and ask themselves what message they get from the building. They then may be able to look at their own church with a greater degree of objectivity and understand what their congregation is communicating through its physical facilities. The building is the first thing a newcomer sees. It is important to ask what message it conveys.

8. UNITED METHODIST POLITY AND THE LARGE CHURCH

Every local church operates within the framework of a denominational polity. Even an independent congregation is organized according to a particular tradition. Throughout history, Christian churches have carried on their work through a variety of organizational patterns. These tend to be based both on the particular denomination's theological understanding of the nature and mission of the church and certain social and cultural conditions in the larger society. The circumstance under which a particular denomination was founded often has a significant impact on the way it is organized.

There is no "right" way to structure a church, although it will be fiercely contended by some that certain forms of organization are more biblical, more efficient, or more democratic than are others. Nevertheless, the form of organization which a congregation adopts and/or the requirements of the parent denomination will have an impact on the local church. This impact may be either positive or negative, depending on the particular situation and how the rules are administered. This chapter will focus on how United Methodist polity affects large churches of that denomination.

Clergy Placement

The aspect of United Methodist polity which tends to have the greatest impact on local churches in general, and the large church in particular, is the method by which ordained clergy are assigned to churches. From its very beginning, this denomination has had an itinerant system under which clergy are appointed by a bishop to one or more churches. The United Methodist system of clergy placement is characterized by four factors.

The first is the appointment of every ordained minister by a bishop. Every United Methodist pastor is assigned annually to his or her place of service by a bishop. This includes those persons serving as pastors of congregations, as well as those in non-parish positions as teachers, chaplains, and administrators of church-related institutions. The bishop is required to consult with the persons being appointed and with representatives of the local church, but the authority to appoint the pastor is clearly given to the bishop alone. In most cases, the consulting is done by the district superintendent who acts on behalf of the bishop.

The second is the United Methodist tradition of pastors remaining in a church for only a few years. In the early days, the circuit rider not only was continually on the road traveling among the churches to which he was assigned, but his term on a given charge ranged from a matter of months to a year or two. As the frontier receded and pastors came to be more settled, it was the clergy family who were itinerants. Pastors no longer traveled around a large territory (although they continued to be officially called Traveling Elders). The circuit was (and continues to be) two or more churches located so they could be served by the same pastor. The pastor could expect to move every three or four years.

The underlying assumption was and continues to be that both the clergy and the local congregations will benefit by relative frequent changes of pastors. Although the pastor is appointed annually and usually reappointed to the same charge for several years, long tenure in the same church is uncommon. A large proportion of United Methodist pastors tend to move every four to seven years. While there will be a few exceptions in every annual conference, such as the pastor who has served the same congregation for a quarter of a century, frequent moves are still the norm.

A third factor is the assumption that a large proportion of the pastors are to a high degree interchangeable, i.e., they are able to serve effectively in a variety of congregations. During their lifetime, most United Methodist clergy will serve churches which are located in very different types of rural and urban communities. It is assumed that the churches are similar and the pastor able to adapt to whatever situation he or she is appointed.

A fourth factor is the expectation that the bishop will have sufficient knowledge of both the needs of the congregations and the skills of the pastors to match the individual with the appropriate church. To accomplish this, the bishop will have the counsel of the district superintendents, each of whom serves as a supervisor of approximately forty to sixty pastors. In large annual conferences, the sheer number of annual appointments will require the bishops to depend on the advice of the district superintendents. The result is a highly centralized system of clergy placement which is to a large degree controlled by a small group of judicatory officials, i.e., the bishop and the district superintendents (known as the cabinet). The lay officials in the local churches can give advice and, in some instances, may exercise significant influence. The pastor may express a preference, but the bishop's decision is final. It is a system which tends to work well for the average church but which may present problems for the unique congregation such as the large church.

Conflicting Expectations

In some annual conferences, there may be a conflict between the expectations of the clergy and the needs of a particular congregation. The very large church requires a pastor of particular skills and experience. There may or may not be someone within the annual conference who possesses the qualifications for this post. When this is the case, it is advisable to search beyond the boundaries of the annual conference.

In fact, there has been a tradition within Methodism that when certain churches become vacant, the search for a new pastor is not limited to clergy in the annual conference in which it was located. Persons from across the entire denomination were considered. These tended to be large urban churches which were perceived as needing a pastor of such unusual skills and experience that an appropriate candidate might not be available among the pastors of that annual conference.

These churches tend to function as if they were part of a denomination which called their pastor or at least used a kind of modified call system. The bishop participates in the process and helped the congregation search for an appropriate pastor. When the pastor of one large congregation announced his retirement, the bishop phoned several staff members of the denomination's national agencies to ask for suggestions of clergy from across the country who might be appropriate candidates for the position. Bishops consult with their colleagues in other parts of the country when seeking a pastor of unusual skill. When the appropriate person is located, his or her membership will be transferred to the annual conference and the individual appointed to the church by the bishop.

The system of looking beyond the annual conference for the pastor of certain churches has led some pastors to complain that the denomination has in fact two categories of churches—an elite group which call their pastors and the large majority who have to accept whomever the bishop appoints. To some degree this has been true, but it also is a necessary procedure to insure that certain churches have the type of pastor they need. It is also true that the lay officials of large congregations tend to have more input as to who will be their pastor than persons in small churches. The members of the Pastor-Parish Relations Committee, and possibly other lay leaders, will interview prospective pastors. Representatives of the congregation may visit the candidate's present church to interview the candidate and to hear him/her preach.

The problem arises because there will inevitably be pastors in the annual conference who feel they should be candidates for appointment to the large churches. Such congregations tend to pay the higher salaries, so an appointment to one is perceived to be a promotion. To bring someone in from another conference may result in resentment by those who have been passed over. When a large church becomes vacant, there may be great pressure brought to bear on the bishop by the district superintendents and by some pastors to appoint one of their number. When the pastor of one of the larger congregations announced his retirement, the bishop commented "There is great pressure on me to name _____ to First Church. He is completing six years as a district superintendent and wants to return to the local church when his term ends in June. I have great appreciation for him and his ability, but I'm also convinced he is not the man for that church."

A bishop who wants to be fair to the pastors in the annual conferences over which he presides faces a dilemma when he is convinced that he must bring in a pastor from another annual conference to serve a large church. By appointing one of the ministerial members of the conference to the vacant large church, not only will that person receive a promotion, but it creates a chain reaction, as someone moves into that individual's church which has become vacant, thus creating a third vacancy and so on. Several pastors will therefore be able to "move up" one step in the appointment system. If a pastor is brought in from another area, none of the clergy will benefit from the vacancy in one of the annual conference's top churches.

Clergy naturally want appointments to the larger and more prestigious congregations to be made from among the pastors in the annual conference in which the church is located. A pastor recently appointed to one of the larger congregations in an annual conference said that one of his goals was "to give this church back to the annual conference." When asked to explain, he said he wanted to get it back in the regular appointment system and to insure that pastors did not remain longer than the normal term, and to insure that only pastors from the conference be considered when a change did occur.

There is, of course, no easy and completely satisfactory solution to this dilemma. What is clear is that *the needs of the church must have first priority.* Appropriate leadership is critical to the effective witness of the congregation. The desires and expectations of the clergy must be a secondary consideration. The church which, for whatever reason, is different from the average, whether it be the large congregation or the inner-city mission, must be handled as a special case. *This is because it is a special case.* To do otherwise, even under the guise of fairness to the clergy, is to render a disservice to both the pastor and the congregation.

Ordained Staff

The effectiveness of a large church depends not only on the senior pastor but on the staff. The associate pastor has been discussed in detail elsewhere in this book. Here we shall focus on the issue of the ordained member of a United Methodist annual conference who is appointed as an associate pastor on the staff of a large church.

Every United Methodist pastor is appointed by his or her bishop. It is also axiomatic that the effectiveness of the large church depends on the ability of the staff to complement each other and to work together. It is important that persons employed by such churches be able to function as a team.

There is a range of practices in the manner by which ordained staff are selected in different parts of United Methodism. Some senior pastors report that they and the laity make the decision as to whom shall be employed by the church. While there will be consultation with the district superintendents and the bishop, the senior pastor will take the initiative and arrange interviews with prospective staff members. When the local church and the candidate are in agreement, the bishop makes the appointment. The senior pastor and the lay leaders select a person they feel is most suitable for the needs of the congregation and who can work with the other staff members. The bishop, while retaining ultimate control, does in fact delegate some authority to the senior pastor and the local church leaders.

On the opposite end of the spectrum are cases where the decision as to whom shall be appointed an assistant pastor seems to be based on the criterion that a particular pastor had to be placed somewhere. Some senior pastors are quite frank in discussing the problems they have had securing persons whom they felt were appropriate ordained staff members. One man who has served a very large congregation for over a decade commented, "Under the previous bishop I had some serious problems; we were forced to take a couple of assistant pastors who never should have been in a church like this. Things are better now, and we can get the kind of person we need."

One church was to receive both a new senior pastor and a new assistant pastor. The new senior pastor learned from the district superintendent who the associate was to be. It was a person whom he did not know, but who needed to be in that city because of her spouse's career. The senior pastor phoned the new assistant and he asked her areas of interest. The reply was "preaching and worship." The senior pastor said that he thought that was his responsibility.

One way in which some large United Methodist churches are dealing with the above dilemma is by employing more lay staff instead of ordained persons. The local church then makes the decision as to whom it will hire. The local church can also negotiate the terms under which the staff member is employed without having the standards for salary and housing set by the annual conference for ordained persons. It is likely that the trend toward an increased number of full and part-time lay staff members in large churches will continue.

The United Methodist system is one in which judicatory officials make the critical decisions as to who will be assigned to local churches. It is a method which has the advantage of involving both denominational officials with their wider perspective and the local church officials with their understanding of the congregational needs. If these denominational officials understand the unique requirements of large churches and the type of leadership required, appropriate staff will be secured. If decisions are made on any other basis than the needs of the congregation, and the desire to witness to the gospel and minister effectively, the probability of the congregation receiving less than effective staff will be greatly increased—and the church will probably shrink.

9. WHY LARGE CHURCHES GROW AND DECLINE

The board of St. John's Church was holding its monthly meeting. George Thorton who headed the Committee on Evangelism said, "Our parking problem is reaching a crisis. Last Sunday there were a number of cars parked along Montrose Avenue which has a heavy volume of traffic. We need more parking space."

"I admit that parking is a problem," responded Bill Evans, the senior pastor, "but it is not as critical as the size of the sanctuary. We have to add chairs regularly at the 11:00 service, and the attendance at 9:00 almost fills the sanctuary. We must do something to increase the seating capacity if we expect our membership to continue to grow."

The long-range planning committee of Trinity Church was holding its third meeting. Jerry O'Malley, the chairman, reviewed the work of the committee to date. "We have examined the trends for the past decade and they clearly show that we must take some drastic action. Our membership has dropped from over 2,400 to less than 1,500. Worship attendance has gone from nearly 800 to under 500. If this continues, the future of Trinity Church will be in doubt."

Bob Evans, who had been an active member for over thirty years, observed, "I don't understand what is happening. We have an excellent facility and a good location. Maybe this generation simply does not consider religion as important as we do. I'm puzzled as to what we should do."

St. John's and Trinity represent two different types of churches, one struggling to provide facilities for a growing membership and the other a declining congregation that is anxious about its long-term future.

Every Christian congregation is a dynamic institution. Persons continually join and leave. The factors which cause such growth or decline are many and complex. In this chapter we shall consider some of the reasons a congregation becomes large and why a large church decreases in membership.

A Fragile Institution

An assumption is widely held that the large congregation is an unusually strong and durable institution. Its membership is in the thousands. It has an impressive facility and expends a great deal of money annually. These characteristics are correct and they represent strengths of such congregations. Our observation is that the large church is a more fragile institution than is generally realized. If certain conditions are met, the church will remain strong and effective. Under certain conditions, the large church will decline and in the process change dramatically.

An example of how fragile large churches actually are is illustrated by attendance trends in various parts of the country. In 1965 the Northeast Ohio Conference had 27 churches with an average attendance of 500 or more; by 1985 this number had decreased to three. In this 20-year period, the number of Methodist churches in California with 500 or more attenders dropped from 62 to 17. The number of such churches in Indiana decreased from 38 to 14. In some sections, the number of congregations with an average attendance of 500 or more increased. Florida saw a gain from 36 to 62; Georgia from 24 to 39, and North Carolina from 19 to 21. Large churches seem particularly fragile in the Northeast, Midwest, and Far West. In contrast, the small, congregation, one with an average attendance of fewer than 50 persons, is generally perceived as a rather weak institution. Actually the small membership church tends to be tough. The small church is a primary group; the members know each other well. Some may be related to each other, members of an extended family. The people have an intense loyalty to each other and to their church. This loyalty will not be shaken under virtually any circumstances. The denomination may assign an inept pastor to that parish, or there may be a period of time when the church is without a pastor. The congregation will carry on. There are instances where the denomination has attempted to close a small church only to have it spring back to life under the leadership of a lay person or a pastor of another denomination who happened to be available. One judicatory executive, who had been attempting to persuade a small church to close, observed, "You can't *beat* a church like that to death."

In contrast, the large church is more dependent on professional leadership, particularly the senior pastor, and the program to retain the loyalty and support of a large number of the members. The entire membership of the small church is like an extended family; the large church is a collection of persons each of whom can know only a small proportion of the other members. Close relationships are formed in groups within the large church. The Sunday school class or the prayer circle or the choir may function as an extended family for certain persons. There will be some individuals who will maintain an undying loyalty to the large church no matter what happens. However, some will leave if the preaching is no longer relevant or if the program does not relate to the situations in the life of the individual or if unpopular staff and program changes are made. Members of the large church feel their presence is not essential to the well-being of the congregation. Furthermore, they will be missed by only a small proportion of the people if they do drop out.

The result is that the large membership church can change rather dramatically and sometimes rather quickly if it secures a pastor who is not able to provide the type of leadership necessary in that situation. Support will not be forthcoming if the activities are no longer relevant to the needs of the members. The large church requires careful attention if it is to remain both large and effective.

External Factors

The growth or decline of a local church is the result of the interplay of a variety of factors. Some of these are external and thus beyond the control of the congregation. Every local church exists within a larger community, so it follows that a drastic change in the community will have an effect on the church. The most obvious changes are physical, such as the freeway which is built through a residential community. A number of residents are required to move as their homes are condemned for the highway right of way. In one city a church located adjacent to the new expressway lost a number of members as they were forced to relocate. Furthermore, the highway created a barrier which made it more difficult for persons living on the other side to get to the church.

Physical changes affect the population and social relationships within a community in ways that are either positive or negative from the perspective of the church. A dilapidated commercial area was torn down and replaced with high-rise apartments. This resulted in a church, which had been struggling, suddenly having a potential constituency living nearby.

The community changes which have the greatest impact on the church are in the composition of the population. When a congregation draws a high proportion of its members from the community in which it is located, change in the type of residents will have a drastic impact on the church. This is less true for the large church than for the small neighborhood congregation. The residents of a neighborhood continually change as people come and go. People die, retire, and relocate and are replaced by others. Frequently the newcomers are the same kinds of people as those who leave. Individuals tend to select a neighborhood where they feel comfortable with the other residents and where they will find persons like themselves.

There are times when a neighborhood changes socially. The middle-class residents may be gradually replaced by persons of lower socio-economic status. The lifestyle of the newcomers may be substantially different from those who preceded them. The well-manicured lawns and carefully tended flowerbeds are allowed to deteriorate. One pastor of a mainline Protestant church in such a community illustrated the change in the type of residents by pointing out the number of junked cars, some of which had no wheels and were being used as a source of spare parts, in the driveways and backyards of the twenty-year-old suburban type ranch houses.

Another form of community change is in the ethnic composition of the population. An area which has been predominantly white becomes black. A community which has been inhabited by English-speaking persons now has a population for whom Spanish is the primary language. The change may be gradual over a period of several years, or it may occur in a year or two. The impact on community institutions, including the churches, is drastic. In one racially changing section of a Midwestern city, a congregation which had once been the largest church of its denomination in the state declined to the point where it could survive only as a subsidized mission.

The neighborhood church in such a changed community must either adapt to the new residents and often become a different type church. Or it must relocate or close. There are cases of all three responses on the part of congregations. The large church is in a somewhat different position because it does not depend solely on its immediate neighborhood for its constituents. Hence the large church may continue despite the change in population, provided it is in a location to which people feel they can come safely. If population change is accompanied by a high degree of social disorganization and a rise in the crime rate, people may be reluctant to come to the church. Numerous examples can be found in the larger older cities of once large churches which have closed or relocated because of the change in the population and social disorganization in the community in which the church was located. In these cases, even the large church will not survive despite the efforts of the staff and members to maintain programs for the traditional members and to reach those who have moved into the community.

A congregation always has to deal with the context in which it is located. Changes in the community provide both problems for the local church and opportunities for ministry. How a particular congregation is able to respond to these changes will determine its future.

Internal Factors

A congregation is not only influenced by external forces but also by internal factors such as how the congregation understands the nature of the church and its mission, the role it fulfills in the community and in its denomination, and the expectations the members have of their church. What a congregation does, and how it responds to the changes which take place, will to a great degree determine whether it is effective or ineffective, and whether the membership grows or declines.

Some churches are established in communities where the factors are conducive to growth. It may be a developing area where new housing is being constructed and the population increasing. The type of people moving in find a church of that particular denomination attractive. When such a congregation becomes large, it is assumed that the positive environment was the primary reason. While a favorable context is an important factor and contributes to growth, it is not the only reason. There are cases of churches which failed to grow despite the fact that they were established in communities where conditions were favorable. In contrast, there are examples of congregations which have held their own and even increased in membership in places where the external factors are not favorable. In these cases, the internal facts were determinative in whether the congregation grew or declined. Our observation is that, while certain community factors must exist for a large church to develop, how the congregation acts will determine if the membership becomes large or remains small.

The factors which ultimately determine whether a church will grow or decline are internal to the congregation. Church growth finally depends on the extent to which a congregation successfully reaches out to others and is able to sustain their involvement in its ongoing life.

Congregations which grow first have a clear sense of identity. This begins with a theological understanding about the nature and mission of the church. The members know what they believe and what they feel God is calling them to be and to do. They are convinced that they know what God expects of them and of their church. There is the sense that God is calling them to specific tasks.

A growing church cannot define itself in sociological terms such as by race, education, income, social status, or even place of residence. These criteria can be used to describe the membership of a church, but they are secondary. The basic factor in determining the congregation's identity is the shared vision and values of the members. Therefore, when persons are thinking about affiliating with the church, they will have a sense of what the congregation is and what it is not. When a congregation doesn't have a theological understanding of who it is, the tendency is to define itself in social terms. An example of this is the pastor who brags about how many of his members are members of the country club.

Consensus on what the members believe provides the basis for the second factor which contributes to a growing church. This is a sense of purpose. Pastors and people of growing churches share a common belief about what God is calling them to be and do in their particular community. The central focus of their attitudes, their efforts, and their resources is on the achievement of that mission. While those in different congregations may use different language to describe their mission, their perceptions of their central task are grounded in biblical and theological concepts. Their growth is a direct result of and in proportion to their commitment to the life and ministry of their particular local congregation in their own community.

Every congregation cannot be all things to all people at all times. The studies conducted by persons affiliated with the Church Growth Movement have demonstrated that congregations are not microcosms of the larger society but composed of people who have much in common. While the overall goals of all churches are similar, the specific programs of a particular congregation will be determined by the needs of the members. These will vary among different groups. The congregation in retirement communities will have different goals than will one in which the majority of members are young families with elementary school age children.

The third factor has to do with the climate or atmosphere that persons perceive exists in the congregation. This is important in growing churches of all sizes, but increases in importance with the size of the church. Lay persons say that the primary factor in their selection of a new church home is the friendliness of the people. They join a church in which they feel comfortable. Their continued relationship is strongly affected by the extent to which they feel loved, accepted, and wanted.

Lay persons in growing churches tend to report positive feelings about their relationships to others in their congregation. Lay persons from declining churches, as well as those who have dropped out of the church, tend to report dissatisfaction or disappointment due to what they perceive is an unfriendly, cold, or uncaring climate in the church to which they are or were formerly related.

People will overlook a number of shortcomings in the church, but few are attracted to or content with a congregation where the climate is perceived as cool and where insiders make no attempt to welcome them into an inner circle. Such negative perceptions about a church can override the other positive attractions, including the pastor and staff, excellent sermons, and inspiring worship services. Similar findings concerning the critical importance that persons attach to the climate within the congregation have been reported by researchers in several denominations, by a coalition of national mission agencies (Joint Strategy Action Committee), and by The Institute for American Church Growth.

The fourth—and one of the most important factors which enables a church to become large—is leadership. We have discussed in some detail the qualities needed in the senior pastor, the staff, and the lay leadership. A common factor in every congregation that has grown is a senior pastor who can articulate the vision and recruit and direct a staff to make this vision a reality. Without appropriate leaders, the small church will never become large and the large congregation will not remain so.

The characteristics associated with pastors of growing and declining churches are not easily identified or measured, but they do exist. Some have to do with subtle personal traits. Among these are the perceptions that persons in the congregation have about the authenticity of their pastor's witness and faith, his sense of integrity, his ability to inspire and relate to others, his skill in enlisting large numbers of persons for service and witness, and his ability to work with a multiple staff and volunteers to achieve the common goals and purposes of the congregation. Then, there is an even more difficult dynamic to identify. Some have described it as "fit." An effective senior pastor "fits" the congregation and the congregation "fits" the pastor. Often the fit cannot by predicted or pre-determined. Despite everyone's good intentions and hard work, some pastors and congregations do not "fit." Sometimes it just happens through the mysterious work of God's Holy Spirit.

In a previous chapter the importance of pastoral tenure was discussed. This needs to be re-emphasized. In one study of more than 500 large United Methodist churches, the pastors of growing churches had served those churches 5.8 years. Pastors of large churches with stable membership had served 4.8 years. The pastors who were serving churches that were experiencing a loss of membership had served in those churches for 3.7 years. Those data show that congregations which are growing have been served by the same senior pastor for the longest period of time. Churches that are losing members have been served by senior pastors for the shortest period of time.

Similar findings have been discovered in previous studies which have included small and mid-size churches. The persistence of these findings among churches of all sizes and in all parts of the country calls into question the all-too-frequent practice in The United Methodist Church of moving pastors from church to church every few years. Serious questions must be asked. Do most churches really benefit from frequent changes of pastors? Is there something to be said for the continuity and stability that results when pastors can remain in a community long enough to really know and understand the people and communities they serve? Those questions are especially urgent in light of other findings which show that the young adults who are the current baby boom generation say that, as they move from place to place, they are looking for persons and institutions that provide relationships that are stable and dependable.

A fifth factor which is found in the large church is the ability to successfully define potential constituencies and provide programs which are relevant to them. People's interests and needs change in the different stages of their lives. The concerns and problems of the college student are different from those of the middle-aged business executive. Nevertheless, the Christian faith and the values it supports are relevant to each. These must be communicated in ways that each will understand.

This is critical for the large church because it can minister to a number of constituencies, including persons with special needs. For example, one congregation established an educational program for children with mental and physical handicaps. They call it GSC which stands for God's Special Children. It serves persons of all faiths. In contrast, the small congregation is limited in the specialized programs it can offer. The small church is a kind of generalist type institution which offers the Christian faith but cannot focus on specific constituencies such as single parents, persons with handicapping conditions, senior citizens, or youth.

The church which becomes large deals with issues that are of concern to the people. The agenda is that of the members, not that of the pastor or the judicatory, or the national church boards (each of which ought to focus on the people). The gospel is brought to bear on the issues with which the people are struggling in their day-to-day existence. The people respond because their church is real help. This can be illustrated by the senior pastor who said that the purpose of his preaching was "to help the people make it through the next week."

A sixth factor in large churches is the ability to recognize that conditions and needs change. Not every activity which once was effective needs to be continued throughout eternity. It is necessary from time to time to stop doing something so that new activities can be started. This is often a difficult process because there are generally people who are reluctant to discontinue a program. They will remember when it was effective and perhaps even when they were responsible for it. The pressure to continue with the hope of revitalizing a program can be intense. Nevertheless, if a congregation is to be effective, it must from time to time discontinue activities which are no longer needed in favor of others which are.

The local church provides the individual with opportunities to develop a personal faith and develop spiritually. This seventh factor which is common among large congregations is done through a variety of methods, including worship, preaching, the Sunday school, and a multitude of study and interest groups. One pastor observed, "We have 107 organized groups in this congregation. They range from those in which there is serious Bible and theological study to one on auto mechanics for women." The church does not stop with providing learning and fellowship opportunities for the individual. It enables the members to share their faith and engage in meaningful service both to other persons in the congregation and to those in the larger community. The members of the large churches are involved in a wide range of service activities. These include calling regularly on the shut-in members, providing transportation for the elderly, delivering Meals-on-Wheels, working in a shelter for battered women, serving in the shelter for homeless men, providing emergency food and clothing, tutoring children and adults, etc. The list could go on and on. What is significant is that large numbers of people are involved in activities which enable them to spread their faith and to assist others. A much smaller proportion of people in these churches are involved in administrative activities. As previously noted, the governing board of some churches is very small, and administrative committees are kept to a minimum. It would seem that the leaders understand that sharing your faith and serving others gives people a sense of accomplishment. The necessary but routine administrative tasks simply do not inspire church members or provide the degree of satisfaction of ministry activities.

An eighth factor that contributes to a church becoming large is utilizing every available means of letting the larger community know what is going on. All available means of publicity are used to get the message across to the public. Many mainline congregations seem to feel that somehow people will find the church and learn what happens there. Many churches have a sign which gives the name, but vast numbers contain no other information as to the times of service. The weekly newsletter does inform the members of the scheduled activities. This provides a necessary means of internal communication, but it doesn't reach those outside the fellowship.

The large church uses the media and arranges coverage when an activity is newsworthy. Various forms of advertising are used in addition to the listing on the church page in the Saturday newspaper. Some churches are able to broadcast their service on a local radio or television station. Others use direct mail; some have volunteers deliver packets house to house. Whatever means the large congregation uses, it is effective in getting its message out to the larger community. This takes time and effort by some person or persons in the church—and there will be some cost. One rapidly growing church allocates 20 percent of its annual budget to publicity and advertising. However, the failure to do so will mean that many people, who might benefit from participating in the church and make a significant contribution to others through their participation, may never know of this possibility. Word-of-mouth communication may be adequate for the rural and small town church; it is not adequate for the large urban congregation.

A large church can never rest on its accomplishments. The urban centers in which they are located are constantly changing. People come and go. New needs and problems arise. Traditional values—including Christian values—are continually challenged. The congregation's task is never-ending as it attempts to witness and minister in the name of Christ.

Obviously the presence of the above factors does not always insure that a small church will become large any more than that a growing community will always translate into a membership increase in a specific congregation. Neither does the absence of these always result in decline. They do represent factors which we observed in large churches which were dynamic and growing. These factors tended to be absent in churches which were declining.

10. THE NEXT GENERATION AND THE LARGE CHURCH

A concern of every generation is to socialize the young so that they will have the same values as the persons who preceded them. Every generation wants the next one to carry on in the same manner, to have the same ideals and to maintain the institutions which those before them founded and maintained. The next generation can be expected to do things differently from their parents. Even when the young hold values similar to those of their parents, their method of doing things will be different and often the source of considerable anxiety to those who worry about the future of the society. Parents rarely appreciate their offsprings' taste in popular music. A generation gap of some degree is a permanent feature of American society.

Church members also worry about whether the young will have faith and carry forward the Christian message with the dedication and enthusiasm of those who preceded them. The youth program in the local church is usually a matter of concern; most of us fear that it is not being done well. Congregations considering a prospective pastor or associate pastor attempt to determine how effective the candidate will be working with youth. Denominational funds for children's and youth activities, such as the camping program, are among the easiest to raise.

While every generation has its distinctive characteristics, the degree of discontinuity between them is probably not as great as many people believe. The generation gap may, in the final analysis, be more a function of age than of genuine differences. Today's teenagers may be more like their parents when they were teenagers than either is willing or able to admit. And by the time today's teenagers are in their thirties and themselves parents, they may be much like the previous generation was at that stage of life.

The next generation is, of course, already here. They are the children, the teenagers, the young adults, the so-called "baby boomers," many of whom are in their thirties, with the older ones having already reached that milestone age of forty. This chapter will consider the implications of this generation for the large membership church.

Interest in Religion

The interest in religion in American society continues to be high. This does not, however, always translate into church participation. The current generation does, however, manifest a great concern about ultimate values, about the meaning of life and of death. One only has to look at the number of books published each year which deal with spirituality to get some idea of the degree of interest in this subject. Surveys tend to show that there is an interest in transcendent values. George Gallup Jr. and David Poling have written, "The young indicate that they want to go into the great places of God through prayer, Bible study and personal discipline. . . . Get used to a new word: spirituality."[1]

The continuing importance of spiritual growth is confirmed by a more recent Gallup survey. In 1986 a national poll indicated that "spiritual growth is named more often than evangelism, supporting community causes, supporting the local church and influencing legislation as the top priority for Christians."[2] Liberals name spiritual growth first, while conservatives place evangelism first. We live in a society which is characterized as secular and materialistic. It is a society which has been able to produce an unprecedented amount of consumer goods and services. The years since the end of World War II have, in the main, been prosperous for a large proportion of the population. It has also been a period when both the nation and the mainline churches have engaged in a wide range of activities designed to affect social change. However, the result has not been the kind of society desired. This has caused some degree of frustration and disillusionment.

The Christian church has always known that what is most important in people's lives is not what they possess. The church has also known that creating a humane and just society with imperfect and sinful persons is an impossible task. This has caused people to sense their limitations and again turn to matters which are transcendent. It should not be surprising that many churches which attract large numbers of persons are those which emphasize ultimate values and the individual's relationship to God. When asked how he accounted for an average weekly worship attendance of about 2,500, one pastor replied, "Our program is built around three things: preaching, singing, and intercessory prayer." Churches which emphasize spiritual values do not ignore service programs and social ministries. However, the people see these as an expression of their personal encounter with God.

Denominational Loyalty

"Denominations" are the way most churches in America are organized. While a particular group owes its origin to certain historical events, such as the Evangelical Lutheran Church in America to Martin Luther and the reformation in sixteenth-century Germany, or The United Methodist Church to the revival led by John Wesley in eighteenth-century England, denominations continue because they fulfill necessary and important functions. The renewed emphasis on organizing churches by ethnic and language groups (Blacks, Hispanics) and the development of large independent Anglo congregations represent a departure from the traditional pattern.

Denominations provide a method by which certain aspects of Christian teaching and practice are carried forth. They allow for persons of different socio-economic backgrounds, different cultures, different races, and different languages to experience the Christian faith and to be a part of the Christian church. Denominations provide a kind of "brand name" identification which enables the individual to have some idea what he or she can expect in a particular congregation. Thus the individual knows what the style of worship in an Episcopal church is apt to be and how it will be different from that of the nearby Pentecostal Holiness congregation. The denominational label gives the prospective participant some indication of what to expect.

While there is still a substantial amount of denominational loyalty among older adults, the general consensus of pastors and church leaders is that this has decreased in the past quarter of a century. Persons who move to a new community and want to find a church to join may visit several before they select one. Church shopping is an accepted practice.

The individual will usually start by visiting churches of his or her present denomination. If none of these prove satisfactory, those of similar denominations will be visited next. People tend to look for a church which meets their expectations of what a congregation ought to be. They will find it within a fairly narrow range of denominations. The Baptist will look among the variety of Baptist Churches and the Lutheran will choose among the congregations of the various Lutheran bodies. The member of an Assembly of God congregation will be unlikely to seek a new church by visiting the liberal United Church of Christ, though he or she might consider a United Methodist congregation.

Church leaders must understand that a specific local church will find its prospective members from that segment of the population who are inclined toward its teachings and congregational style. Not every church will appeal to all people; however, individuals will usually be able to find a congregation of their present or similar denomination which will prove satisfactory.

People tend to develop habits of church attendance and expectations when they are young. These patterns may be retained throughout their lives. With an increasingly greater proportion of the population growing up in urban areas, a larger number of potential church members will have participated in larger congregations. As they move to new communities these persons will be more likely to seek large congregations because that is where they had their religious training and experiences. The large church will continue to have a greater advantage in attracting people in the future than in the past when more persons grew up in small towns and rural areas and then moved to the cities.

Expectations of Members

Church members expect that their experience in a local church will be meaningful. They must feel that whatever happens there is important to them. The church is a voluntary organization, so the people who participate must be convinced that it is worth their time, talent, and resources. The expectations people have of social institutions has increased greatly in the past generation. These include the public school, the welfare department, the city government, and the Christian church. A congregation cannot assume the loyalty and participation of members if it does not continue to meet their needs. The present generation is not one which remembers rural and small town America with nostalgia or whose religious experience began in the little brown church in the wildwood.

There is always a corps of loyal persons who will come and support a church no matter what the circumstances may be at a particular time. Studies of congregations reveal that members tend to vote with their feet and pocketbooks concerning how they feel about their church. An inept preacher or an internal conflict may result in lower attendance. Members may not transfer to another church—at least during the early part of such a pastor's stay—but they will attend less frequently and may not renew their pledge or at least not increase it. The laity seem to have an increasingly low tolerance for incompetent or ineffective leadership, a phenomenon that can be expected to continue.

People have different needs at different times in their lives. The teenager is struggling with the decision as to which direction his or her life should take. Young married adults are starting families and need all the help they can get in raising their children. Other families must deal with an aging and increasingly infirm parent. At some point everyone faces the issues around aging and retirement. It is not unreasonable for people to expect their church to assist them in dealing with the problems they face. The task of the church is to bring to the members the resources of the Christian faith as they deal with matters that arise at different stages of their lives.

The large church is likely to have the resources to help the people deal with a variety of issues. Resources not only include the members of the church staff but the people themselves. There will be enough teenagers to have a youth program and skilled counselors to give leadership. There may be enough single parents to form an organization which can focus on matters important to them. The same will be true for parents of young children and for senior citizens. While no local church can deal with everything, the large congregation is in a unique position to be able to assist the members and address the needs which arise at different stages of their lives.

Availability of Volunteers

Much of the work of the local church has traditionally been carried on by volunteers. These are the people who teach the Sunday school classes, serve on the various administrative bodies, sing in the choirs, visit the shut-ins, prepare and serve the meals, and do the hundreds of tasks which make the ministry of the local church possible.

While the church will continue to receive a great deal of volunteer service, the amount of time has decreased for some members. Much of the volunteer work traditionally has been done by women who did not work outside the home. With the increase in the number of employed women, fewer have the same amount of free time to give to the church than was the case a generation ago.

In 1950 only 12 percent of married women living with their husband and at least one child under six were employed outside the home; in 1986 the proportion was 51 percent. Among women with older children the proportion employed is higher. In 1950 there were 28 percent of married women with a husband and children between the ages of 6 and 17 employed outside the home; in 1983 this proportion had increased to 63 percent.[3]

The increase in the number of employed women has affected all organizations which depend heavily on volunteers. Its impact on The United Methodist Church can be noted in the total number of members in the United Methodist Women, an organization which *The Discipline* mandates that each local congregation shall have. In 1973 the women's organization had a total of 1,398,741 members in the local chapters; by 1986 this figure had decreased to 1,165,879 for a loss of 16.6 percent.[4] During the 13-year period, the number of members decreased by 232,862 or an average of 17,912 each year. For whatever reasons, the United Methodist Women's group, is less attractive to women born after 1950.

The decrease in the availability of volunteers has a lesser impact on large churches than on small. First, a large church will have a paid professional staff; the small one may have only the pastor. There will be more persons employed by the church to give direction and leadership to the program. Second, and more important, a large congregation will have a bigger pool from which to draw volunteers. It is, therefore, more likely to have enough people with the time and ability to staff the committees and carry on the various ministries of the congregation than does the small membership church.

The Pastor's Task

In a world of increasing specialization, the pastor remains a generalist. Every pastor is expected to be competent in several diverse areas. He or she is expected to be the resident theologian, biblical scholar, preacher, worship leader, religious educator, pastoral counselor, administrator, and fund raiser. It is self-evident that each pastor will have greater skills in some areas than others. While all must perform in each area, individuals will tend to put time and energy into those functions in which they have interest and ability.

The church with one pastor and no staff cannot provide the specialized activities designed to meet the particular needs of the members. The small church has preaching, worship, and an educational program. Occasionally a congregation will engage in a specialized activity, but usually there is little time or resources to do much beyond the basics.

Furthermore, the pastor of the small church is the only professional program leader the congregation has. A large portion of the budget is earmarked for his or her salary. Some small churches spend well over half of their income to support the pastor. Raising enough funds to employ a pastor is an increasing problem for small churches. The ministry is a labor-intensive occupation; there is little that can be done to speed up the pastor's task. Unlike for the factory worker, automated equipment cannot be secured to increase productivity without raising labor costs. A call on someone in the hospital or the preparation of a sermon cannot be speeded up. If the pastor is to receive a raise, the members must provide more funds. Some denominations have devised complex systems of salary subsidy. These tend to be stop-gap measures which provide only temporary relief.

A large number of churches will continue as institutions with one pastor. Both the clergy and the denominational officials must realize that an increasing proportion of members will be in large churches. When this is recognized, steps can be taken to see that clergy and ordained and lay staff members needed by such congregations are identified, trained, and placed. The role of the specialist in the ministry must be understood if the church is to serve the increasingly diverse groups in American society. Currently the generalist tends to be considered the norm. This is an attitude which should be challenged in the period ahead.

Small and Large Churches

Not all Christians prefer to participate in a large membership church. The existence of many small congregations attests to this fact. While a large proportion of these are in sparsely populated rural areas and small towns, many are in large cities where persons could attend large congregations if they were inclined to do so. The small church offers the participant certain things, such as an opportunity to know everyone, to feel a part of the total group, and to have a say in how the congregation is run.

Small and large congregations are very different types of institutions—and in more ways than simply number of members. The form of organization, the type of program, the style of worship and the way the members relate to the pastor are different. This is not to say that one is better or worse or more effective or ineffective than the other, only that they are different.

One can hear the Christian gospel in a wide variety of settings which may range from the testimony of a single individual to a sermon preached to several thousand persons. The individual can study the tenets of the Christian faith alone or in company with many other persons. The type of religious activities which individuals find meaningful will also vary widely, depending on both their theological assumptions and cultural values.

There is no basic theological difference between the small and the large church. If the church is defined as where the gospel is preached and the sacraments duly administered, it should be obvious that these functions can take place in groups of all sizes. The differences between small and large congregations are sociological, not theological. For some persons, a particular size congregation is not only more desired but more effective.

Our position is that, in this present time and in the years immediately ahead, the large membership church is going to be the type of institution which will be most effective in communicating the gospel to large numbers of people and enlisting them in service to others in the name of Christ. The increasing concentration of people in urban centers, the experience which many persons have had with other large institutions, and the rising expectations people have for a range of activities are but a few of the reasons for this assumption.

Denominational executives will find themselves under conflicting pressures. One will be to provide support for the maintenance of many small congregations; the other will be to give attention to the development of churches which can become large. Both are important, but resources of time, money, and personnel are always finite. Some difficult decisions on priorities will have to be made in the period ahead.

NOTES

1. George Gallup, Jr. and David Poling, *The Search for America's Faith* (Abingdon, 1980), p. 34.

2. "Spiritual Growth Seen as Top Priority for Christians," *Emerging Trends* (Princeton Religion Research Center, Vol. 8, No. 8, October 1986), p. 1.

3. Lyle E. Schaller, *It's a Different World* (Abingdon, 1987), p. 147.

4. *General Minutes of the Annual Conference of The United Methodist Church* (General Council on Finance and Administration), 1974 and 1987 editions.

11. CRITICAL QUESTIONS REGARDING THE LARGE CHURCH

The questions which a group addresses indicate the direction the group is going to take. What we ask determines what we think is important. To some degree, the types of questions raised limit the answers and the course of action based on those answers. The large membership church will be an increasingly important institution in witnessing to the Christian faith and serving in the name of Christ in the period ahead. It is, therefore, critical that those responsible for the large churches—lay persons, pastors, and denominational officials—ask the relevant questions. In this final chapter we suggest several.

Can Large Churches Be Planned?

The question whether large membership churches can be planned at the time a congregation is established is both important and difficult. The answer is yes—but only up to a point. The growth of a church—or the lack thereof—depends on a complex set of factors which cannot be completely predicted or controlled. Those responsible for establishing a new church can maximize the conditions which can result in growth. For example, the site can be accessible, visible, and in an area where population growth is anticipated. It can be large enough for the facilities that will eventually be needed. A pastor who has the potential for developing and serving a large church can be secured. And the church can be started to coincide with the growth of the community.

Obviously not all the right conditions can be met in most cases. The new congregation must, however, be given the best possible start if it is to grow. Actions which will limit growth must be avoided. The judicatory paid dearly when it accepted the gift of a tiny site on a dead-end street to save money. After nine years the congregation was still unable to afford the services of a full-time pastor.

Denominational executives and judicatory agencies play a major role in the establishment of new congregations. As a rule, the decision to organize a congregation does not come from the residents who decide that they want a Baptist or a Presbyterian church in their community. Instead it is the judicatory officials who may conduct a feasibility study and determine that a church is needed in a particular area. This is followed by securing a pastor whose responsibility is to recruit members and organize the congregation. The denomination must provide the pastor's salary until a sufficient number of members is secured to enable the local group to do so. The denomination may further assist by purchasing or assisting with the purchase of the building either in the form of a direct grant or a loan. The fact is that the judicatory officials have a great influence on the type of new churches that are being established.

It is, therefore, of critical importance that these persons have a vision of what the church they are helping to establish can become. Their concept of what a particular church ought to be will influence the decisions which are made at the critical times. If a congregation is organized on the assumption that it will be a small or medium-sized church, it is likely to be. Not every new church will develop a large membership, but unless appropriate provisions are made at the time of organization, the congregation will remain small.

Can Different Institutional Norms Be Accepted?

Within the Christian church are two conflicting pressures. The first is the pressure to conform to the institutional norms, to follow the prescribed course of action set forth by denominational governing bodies. A regional judicatory embarks on a capital funds campaign and directs that each congregation solicit pledges from its members at the same time and in conjunction with the annual drive to underwrite the local church budget. Denominational programs carry the expectation of participation by each local church. The second and opposite pressure is to minister to the particular needs of the people in the congregation and the community. This is with the clear recognition that the required ministries will vary widely among different groups of people. To serve effectively may require some deviation from the denominational norms, doing things differently, and even allocating some resources to untried and experimental programs which, by their very nature, carry the risk of failure.

The development of large membership churches will require some departure from the accepted way of doing things. It should be remembered that the vast majority of congregations are small to medium-sized. It is the pastors and lay representatives of these churches who make up the predominant number of voters in the judicatories. The normal tendency is to give attention to the more "average" congregation.

If large membership churches are to be developed in the mainline denominations, the fact that they will function somewhat differently must be accepted. The unique role of such churches should be affirmed and strengthened. One example is in the area of pastoral leadership. There is great pressure in The United Methodist Church to select pastors for large congregations only from among the ministerial members of the annual conference in which the church is located. Some have this as a stated policy. This assures promotions not only for the pastor selected for the large church but for several others who move up a step as a series of vacancies occurs. Of course, there may be a pastor within the annual conference with appropriate talents for the position who should be named to the post. However, by limiting the potential candidates, a congregation may be deprived of the best person.

Another factor is the tenure of the senior pastor. Large churches tend to be developed under the leadership of a particular individual. An itinerant system with frequent moves may be disfunctional to the development of large churches.

A large membership church will tend to have a degree of independence and not always follow the denominational program. One senior pastor put it this way: "We use whatever materials and resources we feel are appropriate to our situation." Staff may develop their own programs. The congregation will provide financial support for the parent denomination, but its sense of self-sufficiency will likely disturb some judicatory officials.

If a denomination is going to encourage the development of large churches, their uniqueness must be understood and affirmed. The action of a judicatory can foster or hinder the development of such congregations. The consequences of denominational policies should be understood by all.

Can Staff Be Identified, Trained, and Placed?

Throughout this book, great emphasis has been placed on leadership as the critical factor in the effectiveness of the large church. The senior pastor occupies the key role, but for him to be effective there must be staff specialists who can give leadership to the management and program of the church. Large congregations require professional leaders with the skills appropriate to the church at a particular time.

The ministry is a profession which is both egalitarian and competitive.

It is egalitarian in the sense that all clergy are expected to be called by God into the ministry and to serve where they are needed without undue regard for the material rewards they might receive. At the same time there is competition, sometimes subtle, for positions of prestige within the denominational system. There is the assumption that the pastor will "move up" in his or her career, i.e., from smaller to larger churches and from rural to urban settings. While the expectation of upward clergy mobility is widespread, not every pastor is able to meet this expectation. Individuals possess different abilities. Furthermore, there are many more small congregations than large ones, so that only a relatively small proportion of the clergy will have the opportunity to serve a large church during their lifetime.

It may appear that, because serving a large church is associated with high status, we are advocating a kind of elitism among the clergy. This is not the case. We are instead urging that the differences among congregations and pastors be recognized and that the skills of a pastor be those needed by the local church at a particular time. This is, of course, the way the United Methodist appointment system is supposed to work, but it is also known that such factors as the current salary of the prospective pastor and that offered by the church, where the pastor is in his or her career, and where the clergy family want to live, can be determinative.

The large membership church requires a senior pastor with specific abilities. Can the denomination identify such people, provide training to sharpen their skills, and give them the opportunity to develop a large church or become a senior pastor of one? This requires hard decisions, such as saying to some persons that they cannot expect to serve a large church. It will require challenging the assumption that serving a series of small congregations is the best way to prepare to serve a large one.

The large church also requires staff with specialized skills. The assumption that clergy should be generalists prepared to serve a variety of local churches works against the development of specialists. The ordained person who secures the necessary training in a particular field has no assurance that he or she will be placed in a situation where the training can be utilized.

Furthermore, the position of associate/assistant pastor needs to be perceived as a vocation in the same sense as the pastor-in-charge. This can be achieved only by the clergy members of the annual conferences. This is the pastor's peer group whose members tend to determine what is the acceptable role of the clergy. If the associateship/assistantship is seen as a vocation, the church will find more persons who have the skills and desire to serve in that position. This will require many clergy to have a broader view of what are acceptable long-term ministerial careers than they now have.

Can Authority and Responsibility Be Clarified?

In a local church there is no center of authority. Different groups and individuals exercise authority in different areas. There are first the required format and restrictions set by the parent denomination. *The Discipline* does this for United Methodist congregations. Every church has a governing board which comes closest to being the center of authority. It sets policies, determines the budget, employs the staff, and gives final approval to the decisions made by the various other bodies within the congregation. The actual decisions tend to be made by the various committees in their area of assigned responsibility even when they are ratified by the governing board.

The senior pastor has authority over certain aspects of the church program. The worship service is an area under the pastor's control. The senior pastor, however, may exercise considerable power which is not necessarily given to him by the by-laws. To a great degree this depends on the senior pastor's personality, how long he has served that congregation, and whether he is inclined to assume such authority. Many large churches tend to delegate authority to the senior pastor and a relatively small governing board. While the basic policy decisions are made by the board, responsibility for the various programs are assigned appropriate groups. The property is under the care of the trustees; the raising of the necessary funds is assigned to the finance committee. The effective functioning of a large congregation requires that the various individual officials and groups not only be given the responsibility for a particular area but also the authority to carry out their duties.

A problem of authority for United Methodists is encountered in the relationship of the ordained staff to the senior pastor and to the Pastor-Parish Committee, the body that relates to all the employed personnel. Two patterns can be noted in United Methodist congregations. Because they are ordained and clergy members of the annual conference, the associate pastor may have direct access to the Pastor-Parish Committee without going through the senior pastor. The second pattern is for the senior pastor to represent the staff with the Pastor-Parish Committee, but the staff would not normally have direct access to that group. This second practice seems to be increasing.

There are advantages to each practice. When the staff relate directly to the Pastor-Parish Committee, the potential for divisiveness is increased. The disgruntled staff member may enlist the support of some committee members. This is particularly the case when assistant pastors feel they do not have enough opportunities to lead worship and to preach. When the staff normally do not relate directly to the Pastor-Parish Relations Committee, the senior pastor carries a heavy responsibility for the functioning of the staff and for the fair treatment of each member. The second pattern where staff relate primarily to the senior pastor seems to be the more effective organizational form.

Whatever form of staff relationships is followed, it must be understood and accepted by all concerned. Only when authority and responsibility are clear can the employed staff and the lay volunteers function effectively.

Can the Laity Be Equipped and Motivated for Ministry?

Throughout this study, emphasis has been placed on the importance of appropriate professional leadership for the large membership church. While the professional staff are critical, the major proportion of the work of the local church continues to be carried forward by the lay members. A question which must be addressed by the denominations in general and the large congregation in particular is the role and task of the laity in the ministry of the church.

It is our observation that the gap between the clergy and the laity has been widening in recent years. In part this has been caused by the increasing professionalism of the clergy. Furthermore, some clergy simply do not feel that the laity can understand or accept current biblical methods and theological understandings. There are pastors who see the laity as hopelessly conservative and out-of-date. An example is the remark of a recent seminary graduate who said, "I wouldn't dare present to my members the method of biblical interpretation which I learned in seminary."

However, more laity are being brought into the administrative and governing bodies of the denominations. The United Methodist Church is an example of this trend, where over the past several quadrennia the proportion of clergy and laity in the various conferences has been made equal. This trend is continuing with a recent decision to add lay observers to the Annual Conference Boards of Ministry, the previously all-clergy body which examines and recommends candidates for ordination.

The tendency to involve lay persons in the administrative "nuts and bolts" aspects of church life is most evident in the local church. The vast array of work areas, committees, and boards mandated by the United Methodist *Discipline* are an illustration. While lay persons should be involved in the various administrative decisions of their church, they should also be participants in the ministry. This means witnessing to their faith and serving others in the name of Christ. One sometimes gets the sense that some of the clergy are reluctant to trust the laity with sharing the gospel, and hence go to great lengths to involve them in administrative tasks.

Furthermore some individuals do not get as much satisfaction or sense of accomplishment from participating in the decision as to what color to paint the fellowship hall as they do in witnessing to their faith or helping another individual. For example, the Sunday school teacher's reward for faithfully preparing a lesson and being present at 9:00 every Sunday morning is seeing the developing faith in the members of the class. Operating the institution is an important form of ministry, but it should never overwhelm the church's primary mission of sharing God's good news with other persons.

If the large church is going to involve its members, it must be in ministries of witness and service. There are simply too many people to have a large proportion participate in the administrative tasks. The effective large church provides a multitude of ways for the laity to serve. One congregation has an extensive program of door-to-door visitation where members call on all residents of an area. Another provides a range of educational, social, and recreational activities for the residents of a nearby inner-city community. These are staffed by lay volunteers, although they are coordinated by a member of the church staff. Every effective large church provides its members with an opportunity to witness to their faith and to serve others through some activity sponsored by the congregation.

Can We Reevaluate the Way the Congregation Relates to Its Community?

For the past several generations the local church was expected to serve the residents of the community in which it was located. Denominational officials took great care in locating new congregations so they would not compete with other congregations. Ecumenical church planning was based on the same assumption; two congregations of cooperating mainline denominations were not authorized to build in the same neighborhood. The ideal was for each congregation to have the exclusive franchise for its community.

In reality, things never quite work out the way they were intended. Some denominations were not part of the ecumenical council and put their churches wherever they pleased. Even some of the mainline bodies did not always abide by the spirit or letter of the committee agreement. The result is that most communities have several churches which offer different theological understandings, make available a variety of worship and congregational styles, provide a range of activities, and appeal to different groups of people.

Large congregations cannot be community churches. They draw people from a wide area because the people find their participation meaningful and appreciate what goes on. Such a congregation has within its membership a wide variety of people, but they come, not because the church is in their neighborhood but because of the church's program. The large church targets certain groups and develops ministries for them which are important at their stage in life. The needs of young families with small children are different from those of senior citizens or young singles or those who are single again. The gospel is of critical importance to everyone, but the large church is in a unique position to minister to persons with particular needs. By meeting people at points where they need help, it can demonstrate the living out of the Christian faith, and bring the individual into the Christian fellowship.

The congregation which is going to be effective is the one which is able to reach out to a wide range of people and to bring the resources of the Christian faith to bear on the problems they face in their day-to-day life. Its ministry will be to the wide range of people who need such help, not necessarily to those who reside in a particular geographically defined neighborhood.

Can the Church Be Effective in the Urban Setting?

The large church cannot be separated from its urban setting. It is a product of the city because that is where the concentration of people are which make the large-membership church possible. The church has always had a kind of love-hate relationship with the city. The mainline Protestant denominations have tended to be strong in rural and small town America. There has been a tendency to romanticize life on the farm and in the rural village. How often has one heard the comment that "the family farm is the backbone of the nation"? The result has been to look backward with nostalgia to a time that never existed in reality.

In rural and small town America, the church has been a significant community institution. In many places it may have been the "only show in town." The one place to go on Sunday or Wednesday evenings may have been the service at the nearby church. Participation was expected and, because the membership was small, the absent person was missed. There was social pressure on the individual to participate.

The church's negative view of the city is not without some foundation. The city is a place where the church has always had competition. It is where the individual can be righteous or sinful without the social pressures which are brought to bear in the small town. In the city the church is not necessarily the only center of people's lives. Many urban churches have had a continual struggle. They have done best in residential areas among stable and family-oriented persons. They have been less successful in inner-city communities and among transient populations and ethnic groups.

The city church must accept the fact that it is in a highly competitive position. It cannot be the social, recreational, and welfare center of the community, although it may engage to some degree in each of these activities. It must realize that it cannot compete in every area and, hence, must have a clear understanding of its mission, the unique task to which it has been called.

The city church in general, and the large church in particular, must realize that it is composed of certain groups of persons within the larger community. It will not contain a cross section of the population but will consist of a variety of people who are drawn by the programs it offers for them at their stage in life or to meet their particular needs. The large church thus attracts persons from a wide area; it is not identified with a limited geographic neighborhood. Its task is to witness to the Christian faith and to serve, in the name of Christ, various groups of persons while realizing that it cannot be all things to all people.

Can These Bones Live?

A question that is frequently asked by lay persons and clergy is whether a declining large membership church can be rejuvenated. Can the membership decrease be reversed and an institution that is perceived to be dying find new life? The answer is a qualified yes. There is no inevitable life cycle for a local church. Whether a congregation grows or declines, lives or dies, depends on a combination of factors. Some of these are internal and depend on the decisions the members make. Others are external forces in the community which affect the church. The members may have no influence over these forces which may have an impact on both their personal lives and that of their church.

There are five factors which determine whether a congregation which has been declining will continue in its present course or reverse the trend. The first of these is the location of the church building. Can the participants get to the church without undue inconvenience? Is the neighborhood perceived to be safe so that people are not afraid to travel to the church? Is parking available once they get there? A large church will tend to attract persons from a wide area of the city. If residents of the community in which the church is located also participate, the opportunity for growth will be greatly increased. For example, a white congregation located in a community which has become entirely black but does not attract black members will tend to have limited potential for growth. The location of the church building is an important factor in determining who might come.

A second factor in determining whether a congregation will grow or decline is the attitude of the members. Churches and communities are not static but constantly undergo change, sometimes slowly and sometimes rapidly. While congregations need to affirm their history and traditions, it is never possible to replicate the past. The key issue is whether the people have a vision for their ministry in the present. The time for which the current members have responsibility for ministry is the present. Whether they see the current situation as an opportunity for ministry or a problem and burden will determine how they serve in the present.

A third factor is the facilities. Churches are built to provide space for certain types of activities and for a specific number of members. Often the building is constructed with the expectation that the membership will grow to a certain size. However, communities do change. Growth in the area may make the small building inadequate to serve a growing congregation and the site may be too small for expansion. At the other extreme, the large downtown church may have declined to a point where the facilities are too large for current needs. To a great degree the availability of facilities determines the program of a local church. Fortunately, most buildings are adaptable so that they can be used for a wide range of activities.

A fourth factor is the program of the church. The congregation must have something to offer, something that people need. This gets to the very core of the church's theological understanding of its mission. What relevance does the gospel have for the contemporary generation? The function of the church is not simply to entertain or even to provide socially useful services. It may do these things, but its task is to proclaim the gospel.

In order to attract members, a local church must define its potential clientele. Every congregation carries on certain basic activities, such as worship and education, in which a wide range of persons participate. It also provides activities for specific groups of persons which meet a need at a particular time in their lives. These may be designed for persons of certain age groups, such as youth, senior citizens, young married couples. They may be for persons in particular circumstances, such as those who are single again or individuals who share a specific need. Not every congregation can perform all the needed ministries, but each can determine what it is called to do at a particular time.

The fifth factor is leaders with a vision of what the congregation can be and do at this point in time. The vision must be shared by the pastors and the lay leaders. Unless these persons know the direction the church should take and are committed to the task, the members will not give their time and talents to new ventures, and persons looking for a church will not be motivated to join.

A Final Question

The Christian church is a complex institution. It has effectively carried the good news of the gospel to virtually all parts of the globe. It has ministered to the spiritual, social, and physical needs of people for almost two thousand years. And it has done so in vastly divergent cultures and under every type of political system. It has survived both persecution and official favor.

The church has been able to develop institutional forms which have enabled it to proclaim the message of Christ and to serve the needs of people in every age and in every situation. It is more than a social institution which is highly adaptable; it is the instrument of God who established the church in Jesus Christ and whose spirit has guided its course.

The large membership congregation may be the institutional form through which the church today is being called to proclaim the Christian faith in an urban and technological society. Will we be receptive to this call?

SUGGESTIONS FOR FURTHER READING

Carl S. Dudley, Editor, *Building Effective Ministry* (Harper and Row, 1983).

Warren J. Hartman, *Five Audiences: Identifying Groups in Your Church* (Abingdon, 1987).

Ezra Earl Jones, *Strategies for New Churches* (Harper and Row, 1976).

Ezra Earl Jones and Robert L. Wilson, *What's Ahead for Old First Church* (Harper and Row, 1974).

David A. Roozen, William McKinney, Jackson W. Carroll, *Varieties of Religious Presence: Mission in Public Life* (The Pilgrim Press, 1984).

John N. Vaughan, *The Large Church: A Twentieth Century Expression of the First-Century Church* (Baker Book House, 1985).

Lyle E. Schaller, *The Multiple Staff and the Large Church* (Abingdon, 1980).

_____, *The Senior Minister* (Abingdon, 1988).

Douglas Alan Walrath, *Frameworks, Patterns for Living and Believing Today* (The Pilgrim Press, 1987).

Robert L. Wilson, *Shaping the Congregation* (Abingdon, 1981).